A TALE OF **TWO TEMPLES** AND OTHER ESSAYS

A TALE OF **TWO TEMPLES** AND OTHER ESSAYS

PRAFULL GORADIA

Vitasta

Published by
Vitasta Publishing Pvt Ltd
2/15, Ansari Road, Daryaganj
New Delhi - 110 002
info@vitastapublishing.com

ISBN 978-93-90961-18-4

First Edition 2021
MRP ₹495

Edited by Veena Batra
Cover and layout by Somesh Kumar Mishra
Printed at Chaman Enterprises, New Delhi

CONTENTS

WHY THIS BOOK?

This is not a conventional book. It does not deal with one subject or a single theme. It consists of essays on events as they took place, or as the developments were perceived.

In fact, the essays weave a basket of ideas sequenced in an orderly manner.

Even if a reader is not interested in all the ideas, she or he would be attracted to some of them.

Another advantage of the book could be that it can be read while waiting for a flight or on the flight itself. In other words, the reading could be adjusted to your convenience without remembering what you read last and on which page.

BENGAL IS UNIQUE

THE CLASH between BJP party workers and the police on the west side of the Hooghly River on Thursday 8 October, 2020, was not unusual for West Bengal politics. But such clashes should not be taken as a measure of the state's political ethos. The BJP means well in desiring to come to power when the next elections are held. No doubt its leaders remember that since the unfortunate passing away of Dr Syama Prasad Mookerjee in 1953, Bengal has not thrown up a single leader who particularly cared for the Hindus. Instead of doing anything to come to their help, Prime Minister Nehru wrote several times to Chief Minister Bidhan Roy. To quote from the PM's letter dated 16 August 1948: "There is no reasonable solution of the problem if there is a large influx from East Bengal. That is why I have been terribly anxious throughout to prevent this, whatever might happen. I think that it was a very wrong thing for some of the Hindu leaders of East Bengal to come to West Bengal". On 22 August, Nehru again wrote: "If that (crossover) happened on a mass scale it would be a disaster of the first magnitude. I shudder at the prospect". When Nehru tried similar arm-twisting on the Punjab, it was reported that his life was threatened.

Ironically, in the years before Partition and for a while thereafter, the Congress was known as a Hindu party. All this goodwill was drowned in the rivers of Bengal. The beneficiaries of the refugee voters in the following decades were the communist parties who had actively supported Partition and, therefore, were a cause of the tragedy. The Jana Sangh, RSS and the Hindu Mahasabha tried hard to be of help to the refugees but in the Bengal of that time, they had very few workers and fewer resources. They were completely overshadowed by the numerous communists. What a paradox! One-third of the refugee voters became the eventual vote-bank of the Left Front. The sun virtually set on the Bengal Congress in 1977, over four decades ago.

For a couple of general elections, the Hindu Mahasabha won four MLA seats but only in Bankura district. The Jana Sangh and its allies could win little electoral support, nor could they field a single popular leader since the death of Dr SP Mookerjee. It is true that Prof Haripada Bharati was a respected person, but he was not a vote-puller. For this, the substantial reason lies in the Bengali genius as well as kindness of heart. Whether Christian, Muslim or Hindu, the people are Bengali first and everything else, including religion, later. For example, to illustrate this contention, the national anthem of Bangladesh is a song written by Gurudev Rabindranath Tagore. Reportedly, the finest singer of Rabindra *sangeet* is a Bangladeshi Muslim lady of Dhaka, Rezwana Choudhury Bannya, who wears a sari and a *tika*. Religion does not inhibit her like many other Muslim ladies in Bangladesh.

The root of the Bangladesh movement was language more than anything else. In February 1948, Qaid-e-Azam Jinnah visited Dacca (now Dhaka) for the first time and happened to address the university students. Therein he asserted that Pakistan would have one national language and that was Urdu. When the audience asked, "What about Bengali? We are the majority in Pakistan", Jinnah was provoked to counter them by asking, "Do you Bengalis of East Pakistan have any notable exploits or achievements to your credit?" The response to this was the first agitation on the streets of Dhaka. Before long, Sheikh Mujibur Rahman, Bangladesh's current prime minister's father, resigned from the Muslim League and inaugurated the Awami League. He led the movement for the assertion of East Bengal and its eventual secession from what was the initial Aligarh dream of not only a Muslim homeland but also a new Medina. The abolition of the Caliphate in 1924 by Mustafa Kamal Pasha, the great moderniser of Turkey was a big blow to the *momins* of Sunni Islam. The scholars at Aligarh Muslim University wanted Pakistan also in the hope of throwing up a new Caliph. The East Bengalis were not a party to these dreams. In fact, in 1946-47, Fazlur Rahman, a popular peasant leader, and Abdul Rahim were negotiating with Sarat Chandra Bose, Netaji Subhas' elder brother, for a united Bengal as a third dominion after Independence. The other two dominions would have been Hindustan and Pakistan.

Most of the Muslims of now Bangladesh were converted by maulvis coming to the area via Chittagong and settling there. These Muslim clergymen had accompanied Arab traders since the 11th century. Except for being formally Muslim, the inhabitants of the eastern part remained culturally Bengali. Many of them wore dhotis and the women mostly dressed in saris. Incidentally, even in Kolkata, Hindu gentlemen wore lungis at home. When referring to the Muslims, the Bengali *bhadralok* often called them *bechara* Musalman. The explanation was that the richer Hindus had exploited and socially discriminated against the Muslims especially in the villages, to the extent that when they were invited for dinner to a Hindu wedding, they had to clear their own *thalis* and often clean them. The servants served only the Hindu guests. In any case, most Muslims in East Bengal were treated like serfs by the Hindu *zamindars*. They never dared to describe Hindus as *kafirs* even when talking among themselves. Most of those who abducted Hindu girls and created trouble to chase out Hindu property owners were those who had come from outside and settled in Bengal. Even today, it is mostly not difficult to recognise the difference between the locals and the once outsiders. For instance, Khwaja Nazimuddin, the second prime minister of Pakistan belonged to a family of settlers whereas Sheikh Mujibur Rahman was a local ethnic Bengali, as is his daughter. But Khalida Zia, a previous prime minister clearly appears to be from a settler family.

One cannot deny an undercurrent of Hindu-Muslim differences regardless of what I have described above. The word Hindutva was believed to have been first used in writing in 1863 by Raj Narayan Bose, the maternal grandfather of Sri Aurobindo. The Anushilan Samiti was founded in Bengal as was Hindu Mela and others. Similarly, whenever the Muslim thinks of the Bengali Hindu and his socio-economic superiority, he resents him. He expresses his resentment by being more Muslim than normally. Otherwise, he looks upon the Hindu as a fellow Bengali. He does swing between using *aakash-paatal* and *aasman-zameen*, as has been noticed in the Bangladeshi media.

Given this backdrop, therefore, it is clear that West Bengal is politically very different from say, the Hindi heartland states.

WEST BENGAL ECONOMIC REVIVAL

IF I were still a resident of West Bengal, my first priority in the coming state assembly elections would be to retain the identity of our state. Let it not in any way get compromised with Bangladesh. We need to recall that on the eve of the 1947 Partition, Sir Abdul Rahim and Fazlur Rahman had come to Calcutta to induce Netaji's *dada* Sarat Bose that a united Bengal should be the third dominion besides Hindustan and Pakistan. The Communist Party, which had earlier wanted the division of the country into 16 nationalities, then began to support the idea of an undivided Bengal. Qaid-e-Azam Jinnah also backed the idea, because a Muslim-dominated Bengal would willy-nilly side with Pakistan rather than India.

When it comes to song, music, language and literature, all Bengalis take pride in them. But when it comes to memories, most Bangladeshis recall their oppression at the hands of the zamindars and their camp followers. Many remember that even when they were invited to dinner at wedding celebrations, they would be asked to sit separately. In conversation a few years ago with some acquaintances from Dhaka, I was surprised to find that they resented that at Partition, East Bengal was not given Calcutta, although the city was, as it were, a stone's throw from Jessore. "Imagine, we then supplied all the raw jute and the merchants of Kolkata got the benefit of all the jute mills and many other industries, plus the great port. It was unfair of the British to change the allocation at the last minute and give Lahore to Pakistan but deny Calcutta to us".

Muhammad Ali Jinnah was anxious to acquire Calcutta and the impression was that he was a capable negotiator. But obviously, he lost out, perhaps because his lungs were failing and his heart was set on getting Pakistan. The interests of East Bengal had a lower priority for him. Incidentally, the Qaid had never visited East Bengal until February 1948. "The only so-called industry given to us," they went on, "was the Sylhet district, which contained the tea gardens." Bangladesh has very few economic means, other than subsistence resources such as rice and fish.

That is why, it needs to follow the Japanese model of importing raw materials from overseas and convert them into products with high technology, for export. It is difficult for many people to have such techno-entrepreneurial genius as the Japanese. The legend of *Sonar Bangla* is threatened because six of the western districts no longer receive the rainfall of yesteryears, and they badly need river water from India. The other misfortune is that most of the land is low-lying and the sea level is rising. According to scientists, in two decades, 17 percent of Bangladesh's land area is expected go below the sea. All these factors make Bangladeshis the highest number of migrants to other parts of the world.

I was happy when a few years ago, Mamata Banerjee, with all the fury at her command, threw a sheaf of papers on the Lok Sabha Speaker's table. She was then demanding an infiltrator-free West Bengal. The state has limited land and plentiful people. The many industries, small, medium and heavy that the state was proud of, have been turned into industrial graveyards by trade unions and poor managements over the years.

Bengalis are gifted people and certainly very intelligent. If for nothing else, for their talent, the state deserves a better economy. A revival is overdue and it should soon be the main aim of a new agenda. Setting up a new industry is like creating a totem, which would have to compete in this age of globalisation with the rest of the world. On the other hand, education is a sphere in which Bengal enjoys a proud image as well as reputation. The first major thrust should be in the field of schools, colleges and universities. Neither UP, Bihar, Nepal, Assam, the Northeast or Bangladesh are able to provide their large populations with quality education. It does not matter if the fees are high, because only the well-to-do would come all the way to West Bengal.

I would begin with medical studies. With efficient management and capable doctors, as many hospitals as possible across the state should be set up through professional managers supported by medicos. Let the doctors do their own specialised work. Management and Medicine/Surgery should not be mixed up. Thereafter, medical colleges along with hospitals should be set up. Significant investment would be needed in creating the medical colleges. The World Bank could lend the money since the government could guarantee the loans. Nearly all the technology is available in India.

There is a crying need not for ordinary schools, but for

excellent ones; hostels would have to be provided. The new Education Policy recently announced should be used as the lodestar for these schools to come up in the private sector with facilities like land being allotted by the state. A similar strategy should be followed for colleges and universities

Next, the government should attend to sub-Himalayan West Bengal. There is space for a splendid international airport in and near Bagdogra, near the town of Siliguri. This is the place for proceeding to either Darjeeling and Kalimpong, or Gangtok in Sikkim. The most glorious mountains in the world form the backdrop of these hill stations. The Kanchenjunga, the pair of peaks which are the second highest on the globe, lies here. Darjeeling is 6,000 feet high, and another 6,000 feet above that is Sandakphu, which is motorable too. One can view the Everest graphically from here.

But for a government to develop this area would be very difficult. What would be necessary would be to persuade two world-class hotel groups and some enterprising airlines, give them all the support, law and order and assurance that any obstacles in their path would be removed in two or three years. Himalayan Bengal would become more attractive than Switzerland. Nature has done its best to give North Bengal landscape beauty without parallel and it is only for us people to make it more beautiful, with facilities to attract foreign tourists. It is, therefore, possible to make a quick start in reviving the economy of West Bengal without unduly large investments but through governmental will and excellence of management.

COVID-19 AND KARMA

IS COVID the result of universal karma or rather *dushkarma* or bad karma? A great deal of thinking and discussion has been done in our *shastras* over the centuries. The general presumption has been that it is related to individual Hindu human beings. People of the Abrahamic faiths believed in the judgment of Jehovah, Christ or Allah after doomsday. The judgment was whether the individual waiting in the grave was to go to heaven or hell as reward or punishment.

On the other hand, karma is the core of Hinduism which has innumerable denominations. Virtually every temple could be a different method of worship to a different deity. Even agnostics, like most Jains and Buddhists are, also believed in karma and its resulting *bhagya* or fate. Deeds lead to destiny; cause and effect. For every action, there is an equal and opposite reaction. No belief or matter of faith can be so close to this law of physics.

Even if we accept that karma applies to all humans whether they have faith in it or not, how can it be connected to this universal pandemic called Coronavirus? Stretching our imagination, we may allow for the phenomenon of collective karma applying to particular actions of a whole community, or that a whole country may be suffering from collective benign or malignant fate. The decisive end or result of a war between two or more countries could substantiate this phenomenon. The good deeds of the winning side are rewarded and the bad deeds of the losing side are punished. Although this presumption is questionable on the ground that many soldiers as well as civilians on the winning side are also wounded or killed, causing suffering to their relations too. Does that mean that these individuals, whether soldiers or civilians, had been guilty of evil deeds and the rest who survived were rewarded by good luck? Similarly, even on the defeated side, there were the dead as well as survivors. What do we attribute their fates to?

The differences can arise on the question of whether death is necessarily a misfortune and life or survival always a blessing. The common or normal answer is likely to be Yes. I, however, do not endorse this popular belief. In all likelihood, the relations and friends of the dead suffer a loss, sometimes irreparable. But for the departed, death is a finality of this life; there is no pain or pleasure to suffer or enjoy. In the event, if he/she has performed good deeds, the next life should be a better one in which case his/her departure is no tragedy.

It is clear from the above debate that karma is not confined to individuals nor is it only collective; it is altogether complex if not also complicated. The subject deserves much more study and thought. But before we proceed, we need to complete the discussion on Covid. How can almost every country be simultaneously affected by the same malaise? Could the people of all these countries, from Japan in the East to Brazil and other nations, including America in the West, have committed evil punishable by the same disease at about the same time?

The only common crime committed across the globe could be killing animals and birds in order to eat their meat since time immemorial. It is true that no country has all people vegetarian. Some have always consumed some meat. If anyone ate the meat of a carcass, it would not be wrong on any moral count. But most meat consumed is taken from an animal or bird deliberately killed for food. Not only that, many cattle are raised, fattened and then butchered as in piggeries or poultry farms. I have tasted a number of meats but stopped after contemplating how I would feel if someone killed my child for his consumption. This consideration nails the argument on whether the practice is a crime or not.

Perhaps it could not be seen as a crime in the times prior to the beginning of systematic agriculture. But, thereafter, the uniformly flat teeth unlike those of canines, given by nature to human beings earmarked us for vegetarianism. The issue is unconnected with nutrition, or else elephants, rhinos, horses et al who live on vegetation would not be so strong. It is obvious that each digestive system adjusts to the kind of diet that is consumed from infancy. There are any number of dogs and cats who get used to a vegetarian diet when they are pets in orthodox families. Humans who are non-vegetarians must be mostly those whose ancestors got used to the prehistoric, or rather pre-agricultural times.

One cannot think of any other universal wrongdoing. What else could nearly all the countries have done, which has brought upon virtually the whole world the menace of Covid-19? Uncannily, it happens to be true that the animal population of the earth has come down significantly, whereas the human population has increased. Could there be any co-relation between these two opposite trends? Curiously enough, the USA, which is spacious, prosperous and enlightened, but a meat-eating country appears to have been punished the most in terms of deaths.

Europe, too, is prosperous and educated but it has had to take a big beating at the hand of Covid-19. Again, Europeans have been traditionally meat-eaters. On the other hand, people in Africa could be forgiven as not all regions have had modern agriculture. On the other hand, the Chinese have been for centuries eating practically everything that has life. During a fortnight's visit to their country, we saw a few birds and animals at Guangzhou, the city which was famous as Canton until the communist revolution that ended in 1949. On a street in the city I saw a vendor selling cockroaches per piece and people buying and eating them as we would eat roasted *chana* or peanuts at roadside stalls.

Probably, never before in history has there been such a universal curse. No doubt there have been widespread epidemics of influenza as the one around the end of World War I and several pandemics of plague. This influenza is reputed to have killed millions of people but it did exclude many a region of the globe.

In China every posh restaurant had large glass jars of water with dead snakes floating in it. That water was consumed by customers for better health. The question is: what is the scale of punishment meted out to the Chinese for these evil acts? They are a great people when it comes to keeping information under wraps. For example, in 1962 when they invaded NEFA or Arunachal Pradesh and Ladakh, China had lost three million citizens as a result of a famine, as revealed by Nobel laureate Amartya Sen.

EFFECTIVE OPPOSITION ESSENTIAL

POLITICS IS the engine of society as a locomotive is the engine of a train. The best of carriages, bogeys and saloons would come to naught if the engine was not excellent as well as maintained well. India has had satisfactory governments but poor ministers. Little thought has been given to the importance of the quality of men and women who should govern the country. Neither voters nor parties nor leaders, not even our political scientists have given much thought to this subject. If the latter have thought about it, they do not seem to have written or propagated any thoughts on it.

Indian elections have experienced positive polling, negative voting, voters choosing with their feet and polarised polling caste-wise or community-wise. People have been heard to say that they voted to feel safe as a country after Indira Gandhi's assassination in 1984. Never have I heard anyone saying that he/she voted to try and ensure good governance although after the 2019 polling, I did hear some Kolkata voters say that they polled for Narendra Modi for he was the fittest ruler among the choices before us, although they did not agree with his party's ideology.

That a successful democracy needs an effective Opposition is universally agreed. To add, a credible Opposition should also have an inner-party democracy. Out of the seventy years of India's democratic functioning, most of the time we have not had a strong Opposition or the main Opposition party has not enjoyed internal democracy. Lately, we have had the doubtful benefit of hereditary parties or family-led organisations.

The flip side of this problem is that most politicians of recent decades belong to mainly three categories; one, family tradition, two, otherwise unemployables, and three, freaks. Most others prefer secure careers or pursuits. Even the financially-secure families do not encourage their offspring to risk years of uncertainty in politics. Yet, it is the same India which sent out its best youth and adults, both women and men, to agitate for freedom. Was this patriotism spontaneous to the people or was it inspired by Gandhi? Before 1920, there was no tradition of such mass participation in the country's political destiny. Although India, certainly its large areas were under the heels of invaders since the 12th century. Come 1947 and the patriotic enthusiasm began to dry up.

Independence from the British did not mean that freedom was guaranteed or even secured forever. We experienced a shock in 1962 at Ladakh and Arunachal Pradesh (then NEFA) at the hands of China. Its extent can be gauged from the fact that the prime minister appeared to weep on All India Radio that, "My heart goes out to the people of Assam". Radio China was broadcasting in November 1962 that the PLA soldiers were looking forward to spending Christmas at Calcutta.

Retaining freedom is more important than winning it. Therefore, the best talent in the country should try going into politics. Everyone will not succeed. As planned, I rounded up my commercial career at forty-one and came to Delhi nearly 40 years ago en route to Gujarat. In those years caste mattered so much that a most generous political party could not allot any seat (Lok Sabha) except two at the most. I, therefore, held back in Delhi and worked here quietly for 16 years and then got to the Rajya Sabha for a part-term as a result of a by-election. I was able to build 49 Sulabh Shauchalayas in Baroda city and in all 88 bus stops in the district with the MPLADS funds I was allotted by Parliament.

In India, members of the elite and intelligentsia often console themselves that politics is a dirty game and good people should avoid it. This is not true. In all my years, I found politics was cleaner than my earlier twenty-five years in business. To quote one example, most of the non-performing assets (NPAs) with the banks are purely business failures. There are much fewer scams in politics. If I did not go further it was because of my peculiarities. I was an ethnic Gujarati brought up in Bengal and I had spent twenty-five years in business with no experience in politics. I could not overcome these disadvantages. We must remember that while business management is a game of selection, politics is one of elimination; in business, one generally succeeds without grabbing anyone else's money. In politics, one wins by dispossessing someone else of his seat. Nevertheless, one's attitude should be similar to national military service; whether one likes soldiering or not, two years are to be devoted to training as a matter of duty. In Britain, many an Oxbridge graduate joins politics as do a significant number of public school boys and girls. True, in the USA it has not been quite the same. When my father was at the University of Boston in 1929-32, he often said he would return to India and join the Congress Party. Gandhi was already an acclaimed leader and yet the reaction was often: after such expensive studies why get into politics?

Our voters should be more demanding and not as tolerant as they often are. Take the issue of dynasty. In May 1981 when Rajiv Gandhi was contesting his first by-election from Amethi, accompanied by a colleague I spent a few days motoring through the constituency. One afternoon we stopped at a *dhaba* where apparently an enthusiastic discussion was going on. The general tenor was how well Rajiv spoke. What chaste Hindi he used, etc. After 15 minutes or so I intervened to ask: what service has he done for the country except flying aircraft for Indian Airlines? One person present suddenly woke up to assert that he was learning his mother's vocation. Don't doctors bequeath their dispensaries to their children? Don't lawyers train their children how to be advocates? At least Rajivji would have to come and get elected again and again to get the people's approval.

Coming to corruption, we came across a lucid explanation on the outskirts of Malihabad in the 1984 general election. This was again a *dhaba* discussion, where one Anwar Ahmed, a minister in the state cabinet, was being praised for being such a good and honest man. One of the participants lost his patience and intervened to say, 'Yes, Anwar Saheb is very upright and honest but he has been a minister for ten years and has not been able to build a house for his family. If a person cannot even do this for his wife and children, what can he do to help common people like you and me?'

What management is to a company and its success, government is to a country. Most of our people do not ponder the country's stake when they go to the ballot box. The debacle of 1962, caused by unpreparedness, needs recollection. The Indian army did not have mountain guns or howitzers to fire in mountainous NEFA. The second batch of troops that were sent up to 16,000 feet altitude had canvas shoes, no gloves, and ordinary woollen pullovers. Nehru after Independence said that we were a peace-loving nation and so did not really need an army; the police were sufficient for our purpose. This same political party was re-elected in the following election.

HINDUS, AKBAR AND AURANGZEB

MOST HISTORIANS have overlooked the fact that Emperor Akbar and his apparently sympathetic treatment of Hindus could have changed the course of Indian history. This would have happened had Emperor Aurangzeb played his part during his forty-nine year long reign. Committed Hindus tend to look upon the former as benign and the latter as wicked, if not also malignant. This, one might say, is an allopathic outlook. On the other hand, if a homoeopathic approach were adopted, in the long run, Akbar's policies would have induced complacency amongst the Hindus. One has to bear in mind that Akbar initiated the tradition of Mughal princes marrying Rajput ladies. He had also befriended Rajputs to the extent that a number of Mughal generals were Rajputs. An example was Raja Man Singh of Jaipur, who fought for the emperor at the Battle of Haldighati against Maharana Pratap.

The Maharana and his clan were about the only Rajputs who were not Mughal allies. Mirza Raja Jai Singh was another outstanding example who fought many a battle on behalf of the Mughals. This faith in Rajput generalship continued till the reign of Aurangzeb. There was Raja Chhatrasal of Bundi during the time of Shah Jahan. By the time Aurangzeb came to the throne, he had no choice but to make use of Hindu generals, as Muslim stars were very few in his military firmament. Besides Mirza Raja Jai Singh, there were Raja Jaswant Singh, Kunwar Ram Singh, etc.

Another of Akbar's tactics was also to have Hindu ministers in his cabinet; Raja Todar Mal and the famous Raja Birbal are outstanding names. As if this were not sufficient, Akbar also appeased Hindu sentiment by replacing Islam with a religion called the Din-e-ilahi. The purported Din-e-ilahi was more of an ethical system. Its tenets were the prohibition of lust, sensuality, slander and pride, which were regarded as sins. Piety, prudence, abstinence and kindness were the core virtues of Din-e-ilahi. Celibacy was respected, chastity enforced and animal slaughter forbidden. Celibacy and non-slaughter of animals were more than sufficient to attract Hindus. More significantly, Akbar decreed that Hindus who had been forced to convert to Islam could revert to Hinduism without facing the death penalty. Because of his tolerance he was so well-liked by Hindus that there are numerous references to him, and his eulogies are sung in songs and religious hymns as well.

Akbar also practised several Hindu customs. He celebrated Diwali, allowed Brahmin priests to tie jewelled strings round his wrists as blessing, and, following his lead, many of the nobles took to wearing *rakhi*. He renounced beef and forbade the sale of meat on certain days.

Akbar was also the first Muslim ruler of Delhi-Agra to have married a Hindu princess Jodha Bai of the house of Amber.

Prince Salim, who succeeded Akbar as Emperor Jahangir, was born to Jodha, and was, therefore, a half-Hindu. Jahangir's son Khurram, who became Shah Jahan, was born of the former's Hindu queen Jagat Gosain. Aurangzeb, Shah Jahan's third son and his eventual successor, was only 62 percent Muslim and 38 percent Hindu.

Akbar's son and successor Jahangir showed little interest in theological speculation. Shah Jahan's interest, apart from governance, was in architecture. In other words, by their relative disinterest in religion, in no way did they contradict Akbar or reverse his policies. Jahangir and Shah Jahan maintained many of Akbar's concessions such as the ban on cow slaughter, having only vegetarian dishes on certain days of the week and drinking only Ganges water. Jahangir ruled from Lahore, Punjab, 200 miles away from the Ganges; therefore, the water was sealed in large jars and transported to him. He referred to the Ganges water as the "water of immortality".

Had Mughal rule continued in this vein, it is likely to have created a warm and lasting Hindu-Muslim fraternity. It is possible that some spiritual figure might have been thrown up to further innovate a blend of the two religions of Hinduism and Islam; Din-e-ilahi was inadequate. For example, some faith parallel to Brahmo Samaj, which is a blend of Christianity and Hinduism. In the process, Hindu spiritualism might have got sidelined by the apparently more modern Islamic theology and clerical activism. But Shah Jahan was succeeded by Aurangzeb, who proved to be a contrast to his five predecessors. At the same time, he was gifted with a number of extraordinary qualities. He knew the *Quran* by heart and had mastered the Hadith as an expert; he was fluent in Persian, Arabic, Turkish and Brajbhasha. He was also a capable military commander and loved power.

It is difficult to reconcile all these qualities with Aurangzeb being an iconoclast, an Islamic zealot and an avid Hindu-hater. Unlike his predecessors, he did not marry a Hindu lady. Moreover, he got obsessed with what he was doing rather than keeping an eye on what he ought to have done. He spent 27 years of his reign of 49 years in the Deccan. In those years, not once did he visit north India. All in all, he happened to antagonise Hindus so thoroughly that it is difficult to meet anyone today who does not take the name of Aurangzeb with revulsion. The Muslims are aware of this antagonism; it is difficult to find anyone with this name or with the name Alamgir, which was Aurangzeb's title. In all my tours and travels across the country, I have found only one shop in a lane on the main Kidderpore Road in Kolkata, where a hardware store is named after Aurangzeb.

Had Emperor Aurangzeb been like his predecessors, there might have been the possibility of the Hindu faith increasing to significantly more numbers. That would have been good for the world and its spiritual potential. This point needs explanation in terms of marketing phenomena, because the purpose of this exposition is not religious, but simply peace for mankind. There is something unique about the Hindu faith that despite attempts by other religions to induce conversion, Hindus have not made any organised effort to convert others. Yet, it manages to thrive. As long as one believes in karma, deeds leading to destiny, one is a Hindu. There are avatars and deities galore, but no absolute god. In fact, the concept of swami (master) and das (servant) was introduced by the *bhakti* saints like Chaitanya Mahaprabhu in the east, saint poets Tulsidas, Meera and Surdas in the north, Narasinh Mehta, Sant Tukaram and Eknath in the west and the Alwar saints in the south. Most of them sang and propagated the message of the single paramatma (God). It was an attempt to take Brahmanism to the masses who naturally preferred simple explanations and specific objects of worship. Philosophical concepts were not for them. In a sum, Hinduism is not a religion but a democratic faith without the structure of a clergy or a hierarchy of authorities.

It is like inductive logic, which rises from the ground and moves upwards towards a conclusion. No premise is given like a single god, a supreme book and a founder prophet as the Western religions prescribe. The corollaries of the premise then flow like sound reasoning. It is like deductive logic. There is no concept such as karma; or every action having a reaction, equal and opposite. These religions aim at organisation, possibly conversion and expansion, which often leads to clashes. This is where the beauty of the Hindu faith stands out, for peace and not for war; for contentment rather than imperial activation.

HALF-SOVEREIGN TO FULLY-SOVEREIGN INDIA

THE FRENCH Constitution of 1791was written after start of the revolution and the abolition of the monarchy. "Sovereignty is one, indivisible, unalienable and imprescriptible; it belongs to the nation: no group can attribute sovereignty to itself nor can an individual arrogate it himself". The concept was first thought of by Jean Bodin of 16th century France to signal the progress from feudalism to nationalism. In the times of monarchy, the king or the queen was the sovereign and generally described as such. The US declaration of Independence in 1776 was the first document to enunciate sovereignty as an essential element of the new state. There was no monarch or sovereign in the New World.

Half-sovereign concerns the quality of effective governance rather than the issue of sovereign *per se*. Incidentally, the Pakistani Constitution states that its sovereignty belongs to Allah the Merciful. But that does not lend effectiveness of governance to the state whether the writ of the government runs to the last mile from the capital to the frontiers or not.

Beyond them, the other countries should respect the state if it is to be called fully-sovereign and not half.

The 2005 incident of two Naga groups ANSAM and NSF blockading Manipur by choking NH-39 and NH-53 in the State is reminiscent of a siege undertaken in war. Instead of calling in the army to disperse the involved groups and restoring the normal passages to and fro Manipur, the government airlifted supplies. Home Secretary VK Duggal (*The Statesman*, August 18) is reported to have said in Manipur on 17 August that it was the State's internal matter. This was rather like the US Air Force reaching West Berlin in 1961 when the Soviet Union had blockaded the city. In this incident, three independent countries were involved—the Federal Republic of Germany, the US and the USSR. In the Naga-Manipur episode only one country, therefore, a domestic problem was concerned.

In the same year 2005, Ms Mamata Banerjee had occasion to throw a sheaf of papers at the Deputy Speaker of the Lok Sabha. The reason was her protest at the way delimitation of constituencies was taking place in West Bengal. In a number of constituencies, she had discovered Bangladeshi nationals listed in Indian rolls. It was amazing that foreigners were being enabled to vote in our elections, was her sharp exclamation.

What was happening in West Bengal was not accidental as it had been the policy of the Congress and the Left Front to encourage infiltration, and thus expand their vote-bank. Had it not been so, how would the ruling party explain its sponsorship of the IMDT (Illegal Migrants Determination by Tribunal Act, 1983) in Assam and being unhappy at its having been struck down as ultra vires by the Supreme Court later?

When Maulana Asad Madani pleaded for more privileges for Muslims, (former) Assam Chief Minister Tarun Gogoi had pointed out the Congress's support for the IMDT Act. Assam was the only state where this law was in force. It was also unique in the world because nowhere does the law place the onus of proving that a suspected infiltrator is really so on the complainant. The alleged foreigner has no responsibility to prove his bona fide. Earlier, the Left Front had said that it was a desirable law and should also be introduced in West Bengal. This was a classic case of India abdicating its sovereignty to an immigrant from abroad in order to enlist an electoral supporter.

The inconsistency in Jammu & Kashmir is equally amazing. Years ago when PV Narasimha Rao was Prime Minister, Parliament had resolved that the whole of Jammu & Kashmir was an integral and unalienable part of India. This included PoK. Yet Article 370 of the Constitution continued right until 2019. The State had a separate Constitution and its own flag. A Kashmiri could freely buy property in any part of the country, but non-Kashmiri Indians could not acquire any property in Jammu & Kashmir. Yet, the government expected people to believe that we are a sovereign state. The problem of our Constitution begins by calling India a Sovereign Democratic Republic.

Meanwhile, the government experienced no embarrassment in negotiating autonomy in Jammu & Kashmir with all and sundry, including the various factions of the Hurriyat who were separatists. The government did not mind the Hurriyat leaders hobnobbing with Pakistani diplomats or visiting dignitaries from Islamabad. Equally irresponsible was the government holding talks at home as well as overseas with Naga separatists like T Muivah. A sovereign state would charge every separatist with treason, try him and hang him if proved guilty.

This is clear from the fact that *wakfs* and Muslim personal law still remain untouched. Collectively, the *wakf* properties represent the biggest urban landlords in India. The demand for the Taj Mahal by the UP Sunni Wakf Board and for Bibi ka Maqbara at Aurangabad by the Maharashtra Wakf Board is on the grounds that these contain *qabrs* or graves. A sovereign state should nationalise all their properties as they are deemed to belong to Allah who is supreme and much above any country. Many Islamic countries have over the years abolished their *wakfs*. According to a former Vice-Chancellor of Jamia Millia Islamia university, Asaf Ali Fyzee, wakfs are a dead hand and utterly uneconomical.

Similarly, Muslim personal laws still continue to be sacred and above the purview of the Constitution. Contrary to the Supreme Court's view, the Muslim community now appears to have set up Sharia courts known as Darul Qaza in a number of States to adjudicate on matters concerning marriage, divorce, etc. There are, therefore, two systems of law and justice functioning in the country, one Muslim, and the other Indian. In the event there is a conflict between the two, the Muslim version prevails. In fact, Article 44 of our Constitution states that 'the State shall endeavour to secure for the citizens a uniform civil code throughout the territory of India'. Seventy years have passed and the citizens are still waiting for such a code.

With the advent of the new government in 2014, the journey towards a fully-sovereign state appeared to have begun. A surgical strike in Myanmar followed by one on Pakistan at Balakot were signals of hope. Years ago, there was an incident when Bangladeshi Ranchers had beheaded several Indian para-military jawans and hung them on wooden poles. There was no reaction or retaliation from New Delhi.

Gunnar Myrdal, the Swedish economist and sociologist, would have liked to call such a state a comprehensibly 'soft' state. But India is no longer the 'soft' state it was six or seven years ago.

PUNISH RAPE WITH CASTRATION

RAPE IS not beastly though it certainly is barbarian; it is an indefensible crime. Beasts do not rape; the male responds to the female who is on heat. There are no barbarians in a civilization or a civil society. Yet India has not been able to prevent rape, what to speak of controlling the crime. There cannot be so many policemen watching every possible contact between a male and a female. If at all, the law courts could move much faster when a case is filed. Even that acceleration will not help to abolish the incidence of rape.

Many a punishment has been suggested including the death sentence. Once a convict is executed, he is forgotten. All that is achieved is that the same man cannot repeat a rape. In my view, the most effective deterrence should be to punish the convicted by castration, a punishment which has been suggested by a few citizens. Its virtues are several. The state does not take the life of the guilty. The biggest motivation of the man to rape is to prove that he is virile, that he can bring a woman to instant submission while giving himself a perverse sense of triumph. The imaginary sexual satisfaction could be better achieved with the help of a sex worker but the young criminal might not know this. The older criminal is unquestionably a perverse maniac plus a coward.

In India, as a society, citizens feel embarrassed but not adequately ashamed. Only a few years ago in Uttar Pradesh, a father-in-law raped his daughter-in-law and the supposed compensation to the woman was to marry the old man. In the bargain, her young husband had to divorce her, which incidentally, rendered her children somewhat orphaned. According to the laws of their community, a rape is severely punishable provided the victim can produced four witnesses to the crime before the *dar-ul-qaza*. How practical that could be is a big question mark?

Over the centuries, India has faced many a conquering invasion. It was customary for the invaders and their soldiers to convert or enslave the defeated enemies, rape their womenfolk and often turn them into their harems. Historically, this happened often enough to reconcile the society to rape being seen as disgraceful, but not abominable or inhuman. Although in the context of the world, we must realise that it is an unforgivable black mark on our civilization.

The sentence for rape in China, for example, is death in most cases. In North Korea, rapists are sentenced to death by firing squads. In Afghanistan, convicted rapists are shot in the head or hanged within four days. In Egypt, rapists are hanged, as they are in Iran, where they are occasionally put to death by stoning (Wikipedia).

It is to be hoped that the Indian conscience will be aroused enough to enable drastic action to be taken. This means not only severe punishment for the guilty but also an enduring deterrence for others to keep away from this heinous crime.

In some African tribes, rape is punished heavily because it is considered a violation of property rights, the woman being considered belonging to either her father or her husband. Strangely enough, the Red Indians of America considered gang-rape as a means of punishment of an adulterous wife. In some countries like France, there is a distinction between statutory rape and rape as it is commonly understood. Statutory rape means taking sexual advantage of a person in a subordinate or a subservient position. For example, an employer forcing himself upon his secretary. In such cases, even at 18, the victim would be considered a child.

My own conclusion is that a rape convict should be punished by no other means than surgical castration so that the guilty man realises (for the rest of his life), his inadequacy and the lack of potency which he was so proud of, and which was the most likely motivation for rape. A death penalty ends with the hanging. The guilty individual does not survive to regret. The rest of the world hardly remembers the particular crime, the guilty or the victim. Capital punishment has very little utility as a deterrent to other young men. On the other hand, surgical castration of a young man will make him a eunuch; he will also look like an obvious eunuch. In the bargain, he would be a walking advertisement for the society to see what happens to a rapist. Chemical castration is not recommended for our country because it would leave open the door for mistakes or corruption.

Indonesia's parliament, in October 2016, had passed a law authorising chemical castration following a number of high-profile cases of child sexual abuse in the country. The first man sentenced to chemical castration in 2019 said he would prefer an increase in prison time or even the death penalty.

The Czech Republic practises surgical castration for sex offenders. The law was introduced in 1966. According to official figures, 85 people underwent surgical castration in the Czech Republic between 2000 and 2011. However, this practice has drawn strong criticism from human rights groups.

Ukraine's Parliament in July 2019 had approved a measure to chemically castrate rapists. The legislation will potentially apply to individuals aged between 18 and 65 found guilty of raping or sexually abusing minors.

Sometime ago, Nigerian lawmakers approved surgical castration as punishment for those convicted of raping children under the age of 14, which, however, needs to be signed by the country's rulers for it to become the law. The Nigerian move followed public outrage over a wave of rapes, which prompted the nation's state governors to declare a state of emergency.

Castration as punishment has been introduced as a law even in the USA. In June 2019, the American state of Alabama enacted a law that would require, as a condition of parole, that some convicted child sex offenders undergo chemical castration. Renowned American media house *The Atlantic* had written: "The new law will mean that those who abused children under the age of 13 will be injected with hormone-blocking drugs before leaving prison". The state of Oklahoma, too, mulled over passing a similar legislation. A similar bill was proposed last year in Oklahoma but met strong opposition.

The US newspaper had added: "Unlike castrating a bull, chemical castration does not involve removing a person's testicles though the Alabama bill initially advocated the surgical approach. Instead, the procedure uses various drugs to render the testicles irrelevant. In most cases, medication triggers the pituitary gland to reduce testosterone to prepubescent levels".

MACRON DEFENDING SECULAR TRADITION

FRANCE WAS once again in the news after the gruesome murder of Samuel Paty, a French middle-school teacher, which happened on 16 October 2020, in Conflans-Sainte-Honorine, a suburb of Paris. Paty was killed and beheaded in what was apparently an act of terrorism. Following this incident, French President Emmanuel Macron paid tribute to Samuel Paty calling him a "quiet hero". He said the teacher was targeted because he "embodied the Republic", because he "taught pupils to become citizens" and "fought for freedom and reason".

This brings us to the nature of the French Republic. Former French President Jacques Chirac (now deceased), during his tenure commissioned an expert enquiry into what precisely secularism in practice should be. The best available scholar was Prof Bernard Stasi who presented his report in December 2003. On its basis a fresh secular law was passed by the French National Assembly in March 2004. It brought up-to-date the earlier law of 1905; since then the French government has been strict about secularism.

The new Act defined three essential principles: freedom of conscience, equality in law for spiritual and religious beliefs, and neutrality of political power. In other words, there are in any modern state three sets of relations: (a) religion and the individual; (b) the state and the individual, and; (c) the state and religion.

In the second (b) the state views the individual as a citizen and not as a member of a religious group. The implication of the third (c) is that religion and state function in two separate areas of human activity. Professor Donald Smith, a scholar from the University of Calgary, has compared the above relations as three sides of a triangle. And the integrity of (a) and (b) is largely determined by the third relationship which separates them. Therefore, for any state to function as a secular state, it is important that there is a wall of separation between the state and the church.

The French law had attempted to implement these principles. It had not abolished the wearing of either Jewish skull caps or Muslim headscarves. All that it had ordained was that the students attending government schools or employees working in government offices must not display religious symbols of a conspicuous nature, which would include even a large cross. There is no restriction on wearing of any form of dress or display of any religious symbols in the country at large.

The State, however, has to maintain absolute neutrality between one religion and another. The French insistence on secularism or the absolute separation of the Church from the State goes back to 1905, when in December that year a Republican Law was passed by the country's National Assembly. Its Article One assures the liberty of conscience. It guaranteed the free exercise of religious beliefs. The only restrictions were decreed in the interest of public order.

Article 2 states that the Republic does not recognise either salaries paid or subsidies granted to any religious group. The Stasi Report stated that Islam is believed to be incompatible with secularism. This was a provocation in the report and the subsequent passing of the legislation. As far as private employers of schools are concerned, the law is that the will of the institution would prevail and not any idiosyncrasy of the employee. The intention behind the stipulation is to ensure that there is no discrimination against members of any religion, so that an employer does not avoid the appointment of a scarf-wearing lady or a skull cap-wearing man. These provisions ensure not only the neutrality of political authority but also the freedom of conscience and belief, as well as equality before the law. The Stasi Report also emphasised secularism as a cornerstone of a democracy.

The rise of Christianity led to the problem of church and the state. The Old Testament recognised the basic duality of the temporal and the spiritual. This is best expressed in the well-known phrase: "Render therefore unto Caesar the things that are Caesar's; and unto God the things that are God's".

Marsiglio of Padua in Italy was an influential thinker of the 14th century. He made an important contribution to the idea of a secular state. In his words: "The rights of citizens are independent of the faith they profess; and no man may be punished for his religion". With the march of time, science replaced religion as the paramount interest.

In USA, however, an attempt was made at complete separation between the Church and the State. The American Constitution contains no reference to God. Article VI says that no religious test shall ever be required as a qualification to any office. The first amendment to the Constitution adopted in

1791 explicitly said: "Congress shall make no law respecting an establishment of religion". This built a wall of separation between the church and the State.

The Stasi report clarified that Article 9 of the European Convention of Human Rights and Fundamental Freedoms does not create an absolute right to religious licence. India never had a centralised institution like the church to regulate religion nor did it ever interfere in the running of the state. Islam, on the other hand, does not separate the temporal from the spiritual. The ultimate evidence of this was that the Caliph or the representative of Prophet Muhammad was the spiritual head and the temporal chief rolled into one. France did not fully separate church and state until the passage of its 1905 law. Today, secularism is a core concept in the French Constitution, Article 1 of which formally states that France is a secular republic. This, however, does not prevent an active role on the part of the state in the appointment of Catholic diocesan bishops. Thus, the President of the French Republic is the only head of state in the world who still appoints some Catholic bishops.

Former President Nicolas Sarkozy had differed from this French constitutional tradition; he saw France's main religions as positive contributions to French society. He visited the Pope in December 2007 and publicly acknowledged France's Christian roots. Pope Benedict XVI commented that it was important to become more aware of the irreplaceable role of religion for the formation of conscience and the contribution it can bring to the creation of a basic ethical consensus within society.

A law was passed on 11 April 2011 with strong support from political parties as well as from Sarkozy. This made it illegal to conceal one's face in public spaces, affecting a few thousand women in France wearing the *niqab* and the *burqa*. Scholar Oliver Roy has argued that the *burkini* bans and secularist policies of France provoked religious violence in France, to which Gilles Kepel, French political scientist, responded that Britain which has no such policies still suffered a greater number of attacks in 2017 than France.

UNWANTED MIGRANTS: FRANCE'S CURRENT PROBLEM

PRESIDENT EMMANUEL Macron must have had the best intentions in mind when he proposed to pass legislation to defend the secular values of France. The Christians see the proposed law as a welcome anti-separatist drive which is long overdue. As the President has said, "Secularism is the cement of a united France". Many others would agree with him. The Americans are proud of the wall of separation that their Constitution has built between religion and the State. But hardly can any Muslim see eye to eye with this view.

The reason is that Islam does not approve of religion being separate from the State nor, for that matter, does it distinguish between any aspect of life and religion. Prophet Muhammad was also the ruler of Hejaz (Mecca and Medina area). His Eminence was simultaneously a trader, soldier and a family man. So were his representatives or Caliphs; the last of whom was at once the head of Sunni Islam and the Sultan of Turkey. There was and is no gulf between the spiritual and the material. Islam is a comprehensive prescription of life and does not permit any compartmentalisation. This is unlike the Bible which expounded early in the Old Testament that we must give unto Caesar what is his and keep for God what is His.

The Reformation, which began with Martin Luther and John Calvin in the 16th century, was possible because it was consistent with what was ordained in the Christian holy book. No Pope then or later stood in its path with any degree of determination. In fact, the first separation in Christianity took place early in the 4th century when Emperor Constantine moved from Rome and encouraged the formation of the Orthodox Eastern Church based in what is now Istanbul. His mother Helena had the church built at Nazareth in dedication to Roman Mary, the mother of Jesus Christ. Hagia Sophia was built by the Eastern Roman Emperor Justinian in 537, which has recently been reconverted into a mosque by President Erdogan of Turkey.

The Eastern Church does not accept the belief in the Trinity of Father, Son and the Holy Ghost. It confines its theology to the first two whereas the Roman Catholics have full faith in the Trinity. In other words, the two Churches, the Roman and the Eastern, differed on a canonical principle. Islam, on the other hand, has not permitted any difference of belief on a canonical basis. The Sunnis and the Shia split on the question of who should be allowed to be Caliph. The latter felt that he should belong to the bloodline of Prophet Muhammad whereas the Sunnis believed that he could be anyone from the Quraish tribe. The Shias fell because Imam Hussayn, the grandson of the Prophet, was denied his rightful succession to his father Hazrat Ali who was a nephew of Muhammad.

What is being emphasised is that there is a gulf between

Islam and Christianity, which Muslims are unable to permit being bridged with secularism. India has had a similar experience. In order to avoid India's Partition into Hindustan and Pakistan in 1947, Gandhi went to the extent of inviting Muhammad Ali Jinnah to be the prime minister of the whole of India. But even that failed to bring about a reconciliation. This was notwithstanding the Muslims having lived in India in large numbers since early 13th century. Until the British began to capture power in India since 1757, Muslims ruled the greater parts of the sub-continent as sultans, nawabs or badshahs. Muslims do not enjoy democracy and secularism as these contradict the Quran, which does not prescribe God and Caesar being given their separate roles on earth.

Sharia or the Islamic law originates from the Quran and is, therefore, indispensible to Muslims. How can a truly secular country have two different laws being followed by different communities? In India, we have the extraordinary situation of polygamy or even bigamy being prohibited since 1955. Yet the Muslim men can have up to four spouses. Our Constitution in its Preamble calls India secular regardless, but that is a different matter.

Islamic theology recommends that Muslims should ideally reside in a Dar-al-Islam or a land of Islam. India or rather the Mughul Empire was a Dar-al-Islam until the reign of Bahadur Shah Zafar in 1857-58. When the Queen of Britain took over from the East India Company, it became Dar-al-Harb or a land of conflict. The Muslim endeavour should be to reconvert it back into Dar-al-Islam; if that is not possible, Muslims should undertake *hijrat* or migration to a country which is a Dar-al-Islam. In 1920, as a result of a feared failure of the Khilafat movement, half a million Indian Muslims set off for Afghanistan. While some 20,000 odd remained there, the rest were deported back by the Kabul government.

It is possible that the root of the present trouble in France is the failure of President Erdogan to take Turkey into the European Union. Had he succeeded, Turkish people could move to wherever they chose and the dream of achieving Eurabia could be achieved. On the rebound, Erdogan turned to dreaming about a Caliphate. Until 1924, the Sultan of Turkey was the Caliph of all Sunni Islam. Mustafa Kamal Pasha abolished the institution and exiled him. Nevertheless, Erdogan evidently is unable to take his eyes off Europe; he encouraged a significant number of available men of any nationality to infiltrate France to kill and terrorise Christian Frenchmen. Little wonder that President Macron has ordered several hundred Imams to leave France. The killer of the schoolteacher Samuel Paty was an illegal immigrant and the killers at Nice were also similar infiltrators. Legalised Muslim settlers in France would be opposed to the killing as a pathway to Eurabia. They would prefer the quiet strategy of big families and encouraging more immigration from say, Algeria, Tunisia and Morocco. The French welfare rules are such that a family of five or six children can sustain a middle-class life without anyone having to work. The government introduced such liberal rules in order to encourage larger white families but they are being constructively used by the settlers who live in Benelux or the thousands of apartments in tall buildings around cities.

This tale of France is not a new one. India went through a somewhat similar experience which resulted in the birth of Pakistan. No one is to blame except the short-sightedness of the majority as well as their lack of will to unite in order to find a solution.

IDEOLOGY SHOULD BE INDIGENOUS

WHILE INAUGURATING the statue of Swami Vivekananda at the Jawaharlal Nehru University on 12 November 2020, it was appropriate of Prime Minister Narendra Modi to tell the staff and students that the nation is far greater than a political ideology. This was particularly necessary as the JNU has been charged with being leftist, socialist and Marxist. There has been a lack of balance even in the ideologies. With hot blood flowing in their veins, some students go much beyond their ideology, and in their excitement go on to wish their country ill. Why wish and loudly threaten Bharat *ke tukde tukde*? How has the country harmed you? It is the extension of your house; it is your greater home. If you really dislike it, go somewhere else; do not threaten its wholeness. In 1947, a similar craze broke India into two.

I say 'craze' because in 1971, Pakistan, after perpetrating untold brutality upon its eastern wing again broke into two. And what have the people of Pakistan gained except poverty, terrorism and possibly further breaking apart? The Pakhtoons, Sindhis and Balochs are all getting ready to follow the example of the Bangladeshis. It was way back in 1887 that Sir Syed Ahmad Khan of the Aligarh University fame first declared at Meerut that Hindus and Muslims are separate nations. Muhammad Ali Jinnah finally scored his goal and at the same time divided the Indian *ummah* into two. At the JNU the enthusiasm of young students has brought the Islamists together with communists despite the two ideologies being the anti-thesis of each other in almost every way. There is probably not a single communist left in Pakistan although Partition was actively supported by the Communist Party of India. In fact, the party began by wanting and propagating to cut up India into 16 nationalities. Yet, the Reds and the Greens are very friendly in India. When I was in Parliament, a communist leader and I sometimes chatted at random in our free hours. Once I happened to raise this Red and Green contradiction with him. His answer was that it was a purely tactical line. If the Hindus unite, with their majority in the country, they could crush us communists, whereas the Muslims, being a minority, could not do so. They are, therefore, useful allies against the Hindu right, was his reasoning.

Going back to the prime minister's point about the nation being greater than ideology, among Marxism's postulates when the ideology began is its firm belief that the nation is an instrument in the hands of the bourgeois to exploit the proletariat and the peasants. Karl Marx hoped that one day the State would wither away, certainly when the workers of the world would have united. This world unity was the central strategic objective of communism; and nations were the difficult obstacles. Leon Trotsky, a Russian Marxist revolutionary, therefore, wanted the red movement to pursue a "permanent revolution" as its strategic goal. By permanent he possibly meant continual. Trotsky has his faithful followers in India in the form of the Revolutionary Socialist Party.

Yet, one factor is common between the Reds and the Greens in that they both believe in their respective *ummahs* and do not waste their sentiments on their nations or countries. There is a corollary of this factor. Those believers in an *ummah* do not hesitate to abuse their nations in order to pursue their personal ambitions. This is precisely what Xi Jinping is doing with his country China. The notion that he is the latest emperor of the historic Middle Kingdom or the centre of the world has evidently gone to his head. In pursuit of his glory Xi has made enemies, adversaries or bitter critics across the globe. Ex-President Donald Trump openly accused China of having spread the Covid-19 virus from the Wuhan province. Xi has been repeating that Taiwan is a part of China and must get ready to merge. Since the communist revolution which ended in 1949, Mao Zedong claimed that Formosa (later named Taiwan) was a part of Mainland China. There was intermittent bombardment with artillery from the mainland. Since 1954, Taiwan has been the beneficiary of a defence treaty with the USA. Between 1895 and 1945, Taiwan was a Japanese colony after it was officially handed over by China. Earlier it had been a Spanish colony. However, after seeing how Beijing has treated Hong Kong, it is unlikely that anyone would like to come under the Chinese umbrella. Coming to ideology, with the advent of Deng Xiaoping to supreme power in 1978, China became semi-capitalist, although the façade of communism is maintained. Deng's famous declaration was 'the colour of a cat whether it is black or red does not matter as long as it kills mice'. The sum of the substance of ideology was thrown to the winds for the pursuit of prosperity.

Josef Stalin had also abused Marxism-Leninism for pursuing his own power and glory. He had to settle for what he called 'socialism in one country'. It is true that World War II was thrust upon him by Adolf Hitler but after peace returned in 1945, if the Soviet Union had been satisfied with being a great European power, as it had been for over two centuries, all would have been well. Instead Stalin assumed all the trappings of a superpower like the USA and troubles began for the Soviet economy which could not cope with American competition. Eventually, the Soviet Union collapsed and broke up into 16 republics in 1991. Was it not the abuse of his power and the country by the vainglorious Stalin and his successors?

Ideology is a European concept. Till date, there is no Asia-born theory of the kind except the outline of Hindudom or Hindutva. Until about the 17th century, monarchs turned to the high priests of Christianity for guidance if and when they needed it. There was no idea of ideology other than from religion. With the emergence of secularism and the advent of nationhood, nationalism sprouted, which was a construct beyond merely the monarchy. Meanwhile, at the economic level, capitalistic ideas grew along with the establishment of manufacturing and factories. Then arose the feeling of factory workers being exploited. In response sprouted various socialist theories and these were followed by Karl Marx and his great thesis of the materialistic interpretation of history. The need of every person was about the same he said. In his words, 'from each according to his ability, to each according to his needs'.

To combat Marxism, those who believed essentially in capitalism innovated fascism. Benito Mussolini of Italy spoke of 'class collaboration'. Capitalism had been accused of exploiting the working class but this collaboration was a middle path. Mussolini used this ideology to grab power in Italy and also dragged it into World War II along with Hitler, whose ideology was a more extreme version of fascism.

KAMALA HARRIS: THE WOMAN OF THE YEAR

THE ELECTION of Kamala Harris as Vice-President of the USA is the ideal way to celebrate the centenary of women being given the vote in America. In virtually no democracy in the world did the woman have a vote earlier. It is also a proud moment for America electing a woman as vice president, whether white or coloured. Even the distinguished Mrs Hillary Clinton could not win as late as 2016. All that remains to fill the proverbial last gap is for a woman to become President of the USA.

For us Indians, too, it can count as a matter of satisfaction that Kamala is of Indian origin. In fact, she personifies a multi-splendoured combination. Her father is a Jamaican black; her mother was a Tamil Brahmin. Her husband and step-children are white Jews. Blacks are the biggest minority in the USA, while Jews are a very influential community in the country. Kamala is a successful lawyer; what more can America want for a Vice-President?

President Joe Biden, being of a mature age, is likely to let his deputy play a more active role than most other vice-presidents hitherto. It is said that when President Franklin Roosevelt happened to pass away soon after his fourth election in 1945, half the Americans had not heard of Harry Truman the Vice-President. Yet, on entering the White House, it was he who pressed the atomic trigger for Hiroshima and Nagasaki in August 1945. It shocked the world then and it took years for even military experts to realise that Truman had, in the process of bombing Japan, abolished the use of nuclear weapons for the times to come. If the horrors of nuclear bombs had not then been demonstrated, possibly the world would have witnessed the use of comparably more horrific thermonuclear weapons.

It is hoped that in the interest of the USA and the world, President Biden will expose his deputy to foreign affairs with a helpful Secretary of State. One says this because there have occurred many changes in the equations between nations as well as civilizations. Everyone knows that the Soviet Union broke up in 1991, but not everyone is familiar with all the consequences of the event. One mustn't forget that ex-President Trump asked Europe why the North Atlantic Treaty Organization (NATO) should even continue. It was formed to defend Europe against a possible Soviet attack. The question today is: defence against whom? Germany is the world's fourth economy but scarcely bothers to look after its own defence.

China was effectively a third-world economy and, therefore, a second-class power. Today it has replaced the Soviet Union as the second superpower. India is coming up to become a great power, even militarily. Japan is gradually freeing itself from US protection and should soon become a military powerhouse. Its navy is already powerful and its air force is also on the way.

Islamic countries taken together are flush with petrodollars and a fairly cohesive group of fifty-four except perhaps Iran, which is Shia by faith and distinct from the Arab and other parts of the Islamic world. Today, the demand for oil is fluctuating. Vehicles have begun running on electric batteries. The USA is itself producing shale oil and importing almost zero from Arabia. As the demand for petroleum declines Islamic economies would decline. Impoverishment often leads to internecine differences. Already there are two camps; one led by Saudi Arabia and the other by Turkey. The latter was a committed ally of America but no longer. Pakistan was for decades a favoured and aided ally that significantly lived off American aid but no longer. Yet, several politicians in USA still criticise India about Kashmir without any clue about the subcontinent's history. Moreover, the Nehruvian era finally passed in 2014 and the ethos of India is changing.

The USA should also take greater interest in Africa. Australia is an important watchtower as well as a growing military associate. Kamala Harris' country no longer needs allies who cost its economy greatly. To keep its industrial military complex as well as its economy going, more genuine exports should be useful rather than exploitative imports which come in for example, from China. So long as the dollar is so popular nothing can go wrong with USA. However, budgetary deficits are not to be encouraged. In the ultimate analysis, an economy is richer by its cash inflow and less by its fixed assets.

Kamala Harris should avoid repeated references to black women. This was Harris' pre-election rhetoric that she and Biden wished to heal wounds and bring together a divided nation. It is true that a portion of America's blacks weigh in Harris' favour. But it is equally true that she is no undisputed leader of her country's black community; her mixed parentage and political posturing to be all things to all people come in the way. Of course, one wishes America's first woman vice-president succeeds, as she has many years to go. She would, therefore, be well-advised not to provoke her country's white population, even by default. They still make up three-fourths of the USA and have great resources.

The experience of the Indian electorate has lessons that may be useful to Kamala Harris. India's Constitution gives the minorities more privileges than it does to the majority. The latter has been divided by casteism with the political parties winning many an election by pampering the former who generally voted in unison. Over a period, the majority decided it would take this reverse discrimination no more and united to amend the political ethos of India. Today, India's minorities do not know what has hit them. After seven years of landmark political change, its members do not know what has happened. The few whites I have met and talked with openly felt that America was built by them, however badly its minorities might have been treated on the way. In short, one cannot win the whites by emphasising on the blacks.

So it's best to forget what politics one might have learnt at Harvard University. Now the path to political success is paved with nationalism, and united will Americans stand! It is imperative that Kamala Harris heeds the right lessons of history.

LOVE JIHAD

THERE IS a special problem in a Hindu girl marrying a Muslim boy. At a young age few think of understanding each other's concept of marriage. The passion of youth leads them to fall in love and possibly plunge into matrimony. The Muslim method is *nikah* which according to the authoritative *Dictionary of Islam* by Thomas Patrick Hughes literally means 'a contract'. Legally, Hughes goes on, it implies a marriage contract. Unlike in Hinduism it is not a sacrament. Roman Catholicism does not permit even divorce. In Christianity, the Church views a marriage as a unity, divine and indivisible. Thus Hindus and Christians look upon marriage as a union of permanence whereas in Islam it is merely a contract between two parties. For the husband, divorce or *talaq* is easy and a matter of waiting for three months after he utters his first notice to the wife.

The celebrated IAS couple, Tina Dabi and Athar Amir, filed for divorce in Jaipur two years after the two tied the nuptial knot. Their love story and marriage in 2018 had made national headlines. A video of IAS officer Tina Dabi went viral with a claim that she was married to a Muslim man and now she was separated from her husband after two years of marriage because her husband tortured her to wear a *burqa,* convert to Islam, read namaz and adopt Khan in her name.

Even without a divorce, a Muslim man can marry up to four wives at a time. If divorces are given, there is no limit on the number of wives he can have in the course of his life, whereas Hinduism and Christianity insist on only one wife. If, therefore, I had a daughter who wished to marry a Christian boy I would have no objection in principle. For a Muslim boy, I would have to explain the differences at length and enumerate the risks she would be taking. A Muslim man, if he is a faithful or *momin*, can bring forth as many children into this world as possible so that at one time there would be more Muslims than the others in the world. The *Dictionary of Islam* by Hughes quotes the Hadith (the second holy book after the Quran) as the Holy Prophet advising men to marry women who will love their husbands and be more prolific, for he wishes them to be more numerous than any other people. That is why some fearful Hindus have used the word jihad in this context. To be fair, every Muslim young man is unlikely to know all this. He only knows that his family would have no objection to his marriage to a girl of any religion so long as she reads out the *kalimah* from the Quran. Thereafter, she is a virtual Muslim.

Before 1955 when the Hindu Code Bill came into being, Hindu men could marry as many wives as they liked and some rich ones went on until they had even thirteen or fourteen wives all living in the same house. I have, as a child, visited two families, one in Junagadh and one in Kolkata, where the husbands had two wives. In both cases, the women seemed to get on well with each other. My own aunt was a second wife. This combined family of two mothers and six children lived together happily near Lonavala on the then Bombay-Poona highway. Sri Ramchandra's father Dasharath had three wives—Kaushalya, Sumitra and Kaikeyi. Sri Ram did leave Sita after his return to Ayodhya from Lanka on the grounds that he wanted to be seen to be upright but he did not marry again.

Going back to Islamic practices, one is the *mut'ah* marriage, contracted for a limited period, for a certain sum of money. Such marriages are still legal amongst the Shias. They establish the legality of *mut'ah* upon the traditions. *Mut'ah*, or "temporary marriages" are continual upon declaration and acceptance, as in the case of *nikah*, and the subject of the contract must be either a Muslim, a Christian or a Jewess. She should be chaste, and due inquiries should be made into her conduct. Some dower must be specified, and if there is a failure in this respect, the contract is void. There must also be a fixed period, but its extent is left entirely to the parties: it may be a year, a month, or even a day, only some limit must be distinctly specified. In permitting these marriages, what was kept in mind was a custom in old Arabia to assign to a traveller who became a guest for the night, some female of the family.

Once Raja Ghazanfar Ali Khan, the first Pakistani High Commissioner to India, was invited to an annual party by the Maharajah of Bharatpur whose Diwan he had been some years earlier. The rule of the occasion was that the guests should be accompanied by their wives. Ghazanfar Ali's wife had not yet come to Delhi and, therefore, he contracted a *mut'ah* marriage for the evening party.

Some Islamic countries have legislated to modernise their

Sharia laws. For example, in Pakistan, the rule governing marriages is the Muslim Personal Law (the Sharia Application Act 1962). In this law, there are severe restrictions on polygamous marriages. To quote section 6 of the law, no man, during the subsistence of an existing marriage, shall, except with the previous permission in writing of the Arbitration Council, contract another marriage. An application for permission shall be submitted to the Chairman and shall state the reasons for the proposed marriage, and whether the consent of the existing wife or wives has been obtained thereto.

On receipt of the application, the Chairman shall ask the applicant and his existing wife or wives. The Arbitration Council so constituted, may, if satisfied that the proposed marriage is necessary and just, grant the permission. Clearly, the *sharia* has been subjected to an amendment. Its crux is that a no-objection clearance is essential from the existing wife. Malaysia, which too is predominantly Muslim, with the *sharia* governing marriage, divorce and succession, has also placed restrictions. A man cannot marry a second wife unless the first wife consents, and further, the first wife has to fill in a no-objection form.

In Tunisia, by a legislation enacted in 1956, polygamy was prohibited and made a criminal offence. The Syrian Law of Personal Status of 1953 made the permission for a second marriage dependent on the proved ability of the husband to support a second wife, while the Iraqi law of 1959 said that there should be some "lawful benefit" involved. In the case of Egypt, a bill which aims at restricting polygamy and the right of the husband unilaterally to repudiate the first wife was passed in 1962. This information is based on *An Introduction to Islamic Law* by Joseph Schacht (Universal Law Publishing Company, Delhi, 1997).

Justice MC Chagla, in his autobiography *Roses in December* had occasion to write: "I am horrified to find that in my country, while monogamy has been made the law for the Hindus, Muslims can still indulge in the luxury of polygamy. It is an insult to womanhood; and I resent this discrimination between Muslim women and Hindu women".

OBAMA, BIDEN AND INDIA

THERE ARE deeper messages in former American President Barak Obama's autobiography than what comes across in a casual reading. The name of his book, *A Promised Land*, although smacking of an Abrahamic origin, actually implies that for the lesser well-off folk, the United States is yet to fulfill its promise. There is no doubt that to an extent Indian culture has charmed Obama for the *Ramayana* and the *Mahabharata* to have found noticeable space in his life story. That he was influenced by India was evident in his first visit to New Delhi, when he addressed the political elite in the Central Hall of Parliament. His speech was predominantly all about ancient India; the path-breaking achievements, various inventions and some of the traditions set then. Initially I wondered why Obama was selling India to Indians, but as his speech progressed, it occurred to me that Obama was telling the Indian political elite how well he knows their country, perhaps a shade better than most from India's political class.

Presumably, as a sensitive and thinking man, he was missing spirituality whether in his brush with Islam through his father or his practice of Christianity. Evidently Obama had understood Gandhi and grasped his most original innovation, namely the *satyagraha*. President Obama's rueful concern for India's future, especially because of our communal divide, in my opinion should be a cause of worry to us Indians due to its intractability for centuries. Gandhi tried his hand at solving this problem but failed, and gave us Partition as his dying present. His favourite *bhajan* "*Ishwar Allah Tero Naam*" left the Muslims cold, for in their eyes, no one can be higher or even equal to Allah.

Jawaharlal Nehru started his speech at Aligarh University in 1948 by telling its students: "Both our communities share a common history, similar traditions and face an identical future". He was speaking straight from the heart but got only a cool reaction from the audience. Thereafter, Nehru gave the community what they really wanted, namely identity. He became the most trusted leader in India as far as the Muslims were concerned. This Nehruvian ideology functioned with vigour until the advent of Narendra Modi in 2014, who inaugurated a new era and whose motto is integration. In other words, Hindus and Muslims must come together on the same terms.

In the recent US Presidential elections Barack Obama did campaign, more as a senior for Joe Biden and Kamala Harris. This gives me the feeling that the administration could be well handled by them. Obama proved by the visit of the US Marines to Abbottabad that Osama bin Laden and his Al Qaeda were a menace to the rest of the world. He would now fully realise that President Xi Jinping is an ever bigger menace. Xi's misadventures could well result in a military clash. In such an eventually, India would be better placed to take the field with America providing as much wherewithal as necessary, thus saving itself the pain of body bags. In any case, Obama's experience and insights would guide a Biden administration and tell it that Asia rather than Europe is the central theatre of world politics. One mustn't forget that it was under Obama that the US policy of a 'pivot' to Asia, i.e. refocusing on the Asia-Pacific theatre began.

India has plenty of trained soldiers, sailors and airmen, but in an extended war, could well need advanced weapons and equipment. The US and India are, therefore, ideal partners. Neither Joe Biden nor Kamala Harris may be familiar with the complications of Afghanistan or the sea change in Pakistan that has taken place over the last decade, from an American ally to an ally of China, to the extent that for the sake of foreign money, Islamabad has had to give up some of its rights over its own territory to its Chinese masters. This is a pathetic situation. A quick refresher of the subcontinental history of the last century should provide a clear clue as to why Kashmir belongs to India and not to Pakistan. Every reader ought to notice that Barack Obama has gone out of his way in his autobiography to say how much time in his childhood he spent listening to the episodes of the *Ramayana* and *Mahabharata*. This, of course, implies his interest in spiritualism as well as in India. This is further evidenced by what he says about Gandhi, his interest in Eastern religions, not forgetting the compliments he has paid to Dr Manmohan Singh.

The Pakistan story has nothing comparable to offer. All this would soon be noted by the Biden-Harris team. They may or may not remember that President Obama had visited India twice and had been the honoured guest at the Republic

Day parade at Rajpath. In comparison, Obama hardly looked at Pakistan. There is, of course, that crowd of eternal hopers, particularly so in the charmed circle of Lutyens who might be salivating at the prospects of a Biden presidency in the fond hope that it would be softer on Pakistan, and harsher on their nemesis Narendra Modi.

But for the dreamers, what Barack Obama has stated in his autobiography would be a sobering realisation. Describing the events that firmed up his resolve to take out the world's number one jihadi terrorist Osama bin Laden, Obama has revealed that he mulled over three options: taking the Pakistani establishment into confidence, which was a non-starter given the Pakistani army's and ISI's close ties to the Taliban and Al Qaeda terrorists (a fact Obama himself states), air strikes to obliterate the Laden hideout, or a commando raid on his compound without letting the Pakistanis know, thus openly violating Pakistan's sovereignty. In a way, Obama has revealed that his then vice-president was against an operation to eliminate Laden, in effect saying that Biden has been somewhat sympathetic to various jihadi outfits like those which operate in Kashmir and Pakistan. Joe Biden, therefore, will have very limited choices; in effect, liberal hopes for a major American policy turnaround have been washed away. One can speculate as to the political significance of Obama's disclosure of his fondness for India, *Ramayana*, *Mahabharata* and other things Hindu. India is now a pivotal power and a major one as well. The USA cannot see a future without India and for that to materialise, Indian civilizational polarization and support to Biden is a must. Let us not be surprised if the coming American dream will have to traverse via India. Needless to add, all this is the result of the efforts of one man over the last six years.

SWITCH OVER TO ELECTRIC OR GAS CREMATORIA

A CLUTCH of houses in Chah Pokhar in Achhnera block of Agra district have turned into graveyards as some families are compelled to bury their departed in their homes due to lack of space in the burial ground. As a result, the dead here are a constant part of day-to-day life. The correspondent of a leading newspaper found women cooking next to where their children were buried while the elderly rested on cots in a backyard full of graves.

With our bourgeoning population, the man-land ratio is worsening by the day. Yet, significant areas are covered by cemeteries, *qabristans* and other graveyards. Each grave occupies at least five square yards or more considering the pathways and margins. In the case of the *qabristan*, conceptually the grave is supposed to be eternal. Long after the remains have degenerated, the land is supposed to continue to remain occupied, presumably awaiting *qayamat* or doomsday.

An appeal should, therefore, be made to everyone concerned

that bodies should be cremated rather than buried, wherever a gas or an electric crematorium is available. All in all, this is a plea to the various governments to discourage Hindus from using up wood and the others from occupying land. The decision of the Madras Cemeteries Board to construct an electric crematorium at Kilpauk has testified that there was no religious obstacle between burial and cremation, at least among Christians. And Muslims are also *ahl-e-kitab* or belonging to a religion of the Book. The Bishops of Mylapore, Madras, have also given their consent for this break from tradition. The earlier reluctance of Christians towards cremations was their belief in resurrection. It was allowed only in emergencies like epidemics, famines or wars. Moreover, cremation was looked upon as a pagan practice; it was the practice in the pre-Christian era in Europe. In any case, the Roman Catholic Church did not permit it until 1963 when the Pope lifted the ban. Incidentally, the legendary Field Marshall Erwin Rommel of WWII Germany was cremated and not buried. Although the Jews have been conservative, Judaism does not prohibit cremation.

Cremation by wood is a colossal crime today against the country's disappearing forest cover or rather the nation's ecology. Estimates of the quantity of wood used annually for cremation across the country vary widely from 12 to 72 lakh tonnes. Regardless of the actual quantity used, it is easy to see what a waste of wood it is. Wood that takes years to grow is blown up in a matter of an hour into smoke to dispose of a body. In the Hindu view, once the soul leaves the body, it is a mass of waste matter. As India entered the tribal era, the need to get rid of the dead body must have been realised. Most of the plentiful land must have been green with a luxuriant forest cover. Burning the body was the obvious choice. The

Abrahamic people chose burial because they had plenty of land but limited water and fewer trees or wood. Moreover, for them, there is a single life which finally terminates on Doomsday. The body is treated with respect even after death, whereas for the Hindu the soul is all important because it is born again and again; the body without the soul is something to be disposed of as soon as possible.

It is not surprising that tradition insists the body of a person who dies during the day must be cremated before sunset; that of someone who dies at night must be disposed of before sunrise. This is logical enough in a climate which is generally hot and humid. How polluted the dead body is considered to be is illustrated by what many a family in Gujarat practices. A dying person is transferred to the bare floor well before life goes out. The ceremonial use of ghee, sandalwood, etc. was introduced to help the priest to earn some money and to enable the cremating staff to make a living. The attitude towards the body is so casual that all garments are allowed to be taken away by the cremating staff before the funeral pyre is lit. True, there is a sentiment attached to *homagni* or the *havan* as an essential part of the ceremony. However, a *havan* in a small container can be performed without having to waste so much wood, which would be some 400 kg at a time. There is, therefore, no religious or sentimental barrier to a widespread changeover to electric or gas crematoria.

Our country is awakening rapidly to the importance of ecology and environment. It is, therefore, surprising that no national leader has taken the initiative and appealed to the Hindus to stop using wood and instead use electric or gas crematoria, wherever available. No doubt water is invaluable and we are threatened with running out of it in the coming years, but equally valuable is wood which consumes water to grow. And as far as land is concerned, India has an adverse land: man ratio and it is certainly as valuable as water. Why waste it on graves? It is unfortunate that gas or electrical facilities are not being introduced with any speed in the towns and villages of India. In Europe, it is reported that 50 percent of the final journeys are performed by cremation and only the rest by burial. Parsis have been changing over to cremation from their tradition of letting vultures devour the bodies.

At the time of Independence, on paper, India had about 25 percent forest cover. How much was the difference between the paper records and the reality on the ground is difficult to say. It is, however, not unduly hard to believe that by now the actual forest cover would be 10 percent or less in the country as a whole. True, poverty in some of the rural areas is so excruciating that the local people have no alternative but to live off the surrounding forest. Equally perhaps, beyond a point, the governments are not able to prevent unscrupulous traders from denuding the forests. But there can be no excuse for the policy not to be in tune with the country's ecological necessity.

COVID'S PATHETIC SUFFERERS

IT IS gratifying to find that the Maharashtra government has decided to give free rations to sex workers during the Covid-19 pandemic. This section of society is in a way unjustifiably ostracised and viewed with contempt. Hardly a day passes when the media does not report one rape case or more. Yet few Indians, social scientists included, see a connection between frequent rape crimes and its alleviation, paid sex, but instead view it also as a crime. With continual urbanisation, families living apart must increase. When most people lived in villages or small towns, families lived together. With joint families, the young man's income was not a pressing issue. Hence, early marriages were more a rule and less an exception. The challenge of sex did not normally arise. It led to the crime being committed largely by perverse men.

Even in those easier times, the contempt towards sex outside marriage was largely confined to the middle classes. Amongst the upper rungs of society, whether land-based or industry-supported, having a mistress was not looked down upon. On the contrary, a wealthy man without a *tawaif* was not usual. In many a social circle in Mumbai before Independence, the measure of a man's status was the quality of his mistress' singing and possibly also dance. A cousin of the writer's grandfather lived most of his life with the famous classical songstress Kesarbai Kelkar, who was a Padma Vibhushan awardee. An incidental blessing happened to be that he was not married. If any relatives dropped in to call on him, Kesarbai would be around like any other friend.

On the other hand, the working classes did not particularly attach any stigma to extramarital sex. If the farm could not sustain the livelihood of a man, he had to go to a city for work. Not everyone could afford housing or even a room for the family. The result was he lived months on end alone. He then found release by payment which was altogether preferable to molestation or rape. This crime is only recently being looked upon as dastardly, especially since the tragedy of Nirbhaya. Some have called it beastly but the writer disagrees. Animals or beasts do not rape; the male follows a female when she is on heat and not otherwise. Whether perpetrated in public or in the family, rape is a barbaric act.

On the other hand, the world's oldest profession is not fundamentally very different from a contractual, as distinct from a sacramental marriage. Only the time span varies; some contracts require payment, called *mehr*, at the time of wedding. An eligible groom is universally an income-drawing man. A marriage is sanctified by either a priest or a government official whereas paid sex is a private mutual arrangement. At the same time, having a *tawaif* was not looked down upon, whereas anything confined to a short duration was deemed immoral.

One appears not to have questioned the Shia practice of *nikah-e-mut'ah*, which has no minimum time limit. Raja Ghazanfar Ali Khan, who in pre-Independence days was the Diwan of the Kota princely state, was invited with his wife to a special birthday party of the Maharajah. As he did not wish his wife to be seen in public, he contracted a *nikah-e-mut'ah* with a lady apparently for going to the party. The Raja subsequently happened to become an envoy of Pakistan to India. Sir Vidia Naipaul, the Nobel Prize winning famous author, is reported to have been visiting sex workers in London as reported by his biographer Patrick French, the well-known author. This was despite being married to Lady Patricia until her death.

The Vaishali-born Amrapali was beautiful and rose to be the *nagarvadhu* or royal courtesan. She was a contemporary of Lord Buddha, who once in response to her invitation visited her house and dined with her. This incident reflects the social attitude towards courtesans in those times; even the Buddha did not deem it degrading to dine with one. In any case, a number of Hindu temples did have *devadasis* who were sanctified by dancing for the ostensible entertainment of the deities. There are camp followers attached to most militaries, duly approved by the defence authorities.

The contempt perhaps developed after the entry of Christian influence in India. The religion has looked upon sex as a sin to be avoided. Jesus Christ was, therefore, said to have been born of Immaculate Conception, free from original sin. The Church might be justified in its contention, but if it has moulded our morality, it is unfortunate especially for women in India. This has been unfortunate for both—the girls who are victims of molestation as well as the poor women who give pleasure for payment. Incidentally, at one time, Europe did recognise mistress saints. Mary Magdalene was one duly respected by Christianity. Or did the prejudice grow out of dread of contagious diseases?

No doubt, a system of licence should be introduced to give the profession due legitimacy. More importantly, the system would help to protect the health of the women as well as their patrons. And, above all, the women would be freed from the frequent harassment they suffer at the hands of the law and order authorities. Strangely enough, it is invariably the women who are arrested and punished. One never hears of any patron being arrested. Why? Because if any law is violated, it must have been done so by both parties. In Kolkata, for long years there has been a locality, off the main arterial road Chittaranjan Avenue, called Sonagachi. There are many houses there that are rented by individual women professionals. There is no particular stigma attached to the locality or the practice. One does not hear or read in the papers about raids and arrests made in the area.

The writer grew up in Kolkata and spent thirty-eight years there. He cannot remember any reports during those decades of either rape or molestation. Amongst the middle classes, there was respect for the female. The most affectionate way to address one, even a daughter, was by saying *Maa*. Was it because most Hindus worshipped Durga the most? In all, there are thirteen Devi pujas in the year. Was the attitude towards women influenced by this worship of female deities? Some sociologists thought so. There is no doubt that Hinduism is about the only faith which bows to so many female deities. It is eminently shameful, therefore, that there should be so many cases of rape so often.

Paid sex has been widely called the world's oldest

profession which means it dates back to many centuries ago when collective human living began. This means that there has been a universal, permanent need for it. Why then the popular contempt for it? Yet quite amazingly, there has been no attempt in India to reform or reorganise, or in any way improve its condition. After all, the overwhelming majority of women go into the profession out of sheer poverty. Where is our social conscience? Why not begin by giving the profession legal recognition and then make rules to ensure health, hygiene and fairness? A number of countries in Europe did so years ago.

DEMONETIZATION

BLACK MONEY is the opium of the unpatriotic who expect the country to be governed without the help of taxes. It is worse for such money attracts even the honest people to turn evaders of tax. Thereafter, the addiction sticks and corrodes the economy to comparative stagnation. But the phenomenon is not so simple. There are several other allies of the black economy.

For the present, demonetization was effective in dispossessing the big hoarders of cash. Many a smaller holder changed his old currency for new notes for 80 percent to as low as 50 percent. Nevertheless, demonetization was a stern warning to all Indians that the ongoing picnic of black wealth was on the way out. The change of notes was a windfall to bankers, their brokers and some business-oriented farmers. Another great service performed by *note-bandi* was to make Pakistani and Bangladeshi printing presses producing Indian currency illegally, dysfunctional. It also was a major strike on funding for terror activities in India. With demonetization, the liquidity with the traders shrank noticeably. That is another reason for the loudest protest being heard in West Bengal.

The 2016 demonetization would have proved a one-time squib had it not been followed by the introduction of the GST (Goods & Services Tax). It is difficult to escape it if anyone is doing a sizeable business or manufacturing or any commercial activity. If anyone in the chain of production of input material to the product to its eventual retail pays GST, all of the rest in the chain are liable to detection, whereas the erstwhile excise duty and sales tax were easy to evade. I have come across the legend of a Sales Tax officer who would return home late every evening with a bag full of a lakh of rupees, only occasionally Rs 50,000. His problem was what to do with so much cash every working day.

Both these measures, especially the GST, have helped to increase my business as well as that of some others I know, merely because many of my competitors were ingrained in no-tax methods. Then of course there was the smuggling of Chinese goods, whose substantial reduction was a boon to our business. There has been super-smuggling, a phenomenon not known to many. Supposing a trader imported electronic goods from China. The container was four-fifths or more full of the real import items and the remaining were low-priced items say, tooth brushes, or merely their handles. The container got through with a low import duty or no duty for an unfinished product part, the handle.

Those economists who empathise with the Opposition have termed the black economy 'the informal sector'. The words 'black economy' are a creation of our own history. Until 1931, there was no income tax and this subject was not discussed.

World War II, incidentally, made many a businessman rich and they had evaded income tax. In 1946, the British Indian government demonetized the Rs 1,000 currency notes. I came to understand the concept at that young age because one evening my father showed the family two of these big notes we had never seen before. Colleagues at his office had virtually forced my father to buy these two notes at a total cost of Rs 1,200. He was to go to the bank and get Rs 2,000 in exchange and make a cash profit of Rs 800. My mother questioned whether this was not illegal to which father replied that either he took those notes or be teased in the office as a saint for years to come! There was another one in 1978-79 under the Morarji Desai government although it was probably of Rs 10,000 notes and, therefore, did not concern common folk.

Most Hindus have grown up to believe that there is nothing wrong in evading tax. The basic reason is that their rulers, by and large, for centuries have not identified themselves with the people. An antagonistic Gandhi told people not to pay taxes. What greater legitimacy could there be for not paying them? Then came Jawaharlal Nehru who said he wanted to hang deviating businessmen by lampposts. He had no clue of the value of business to an economy. Thereafter, he introduced progressive taxation in line with his socialist beliefs. Nehru went on invite one Prof Nicholas Kaldor, an expert on taxation. He studied the Indian situation and the Nehruvian intention to recommend a total of 50 percent tax on income. The choice of various types of taxes was left to the government. In practice, in the name of Kaldor, nearly all variety of taxes were introduced. The highest total rate for a wealthy assesse came to 91 percent of his income/wealth.

Corporate tax or tax on companies also became high. Private

limited companies had to pay minimum rate of 65 percent of their annual profit. This made many businessmen spend freely and even waste money. Others manipulated to evade taxation. No one in the government had the courage to point out that this policy would strangulate the growth of companies and, in turn, the economy. The black economy flourished with the help of tax-evaded money. The growth rate used to hover around 3 percent which a secular economist dubbed the Hindu rate of growth. Why run down Hindus when Nehru had described himself as culturally a Muslim and a Hindu by accident?

There were some thinking people who believed that they had the ability and the opportunity to become richer, and evidently their karmas enabled them to be so. Who was the government to come in the way by taking away such a large part of their earnings? Thus, they spiritually justified their siphoning off as much of their incomes as possible away from taxation. Such activities were not confined to income tax but also extended to indirect taxes such as excise duty and sales tax. There were cases of clearances at night of manufactured goods without paying duties to the excise staff present and also their seniors. Once the goods were well outside the factory gate, who was to know?

A great proportion of such money did not stay in the country for fear of being detected. It was sent overseas by means of *hawala*, through a chain of specialised couriers whose whole-time business was transfer of money for a commission. There were any number of tax-free destinations where there were banks and supporting brokers who helped to safe-keep the money. They could set up companies for the owners of the money. If the names needed to be secret, the bank accounts were numbered without names. If the owners of newly-formed companies needed to be kept secret, the scripts issued were bearer shares, which had no name of the shareholders. Whoever, other than the banks, had possession of the shares were deemed the owners. They sold and bought merely by payment without any transfer forms.

It was to this extent that tax evasion went. How could the economy really grow? But it stumbled along with the help of even the black money that stayed in the country. It helped in building of property for example. The Planning Commission sanctioned large sums annually to the State in exchange of bouquets of flowers from the Chief Minister to the Vice-Chairman of Yojana Bhavan. Thereafter, what happened to those funds was anyone's guess. The Commission or its officials had no responsibility to ensure or check that the sanctioned funds were utilised. That was the duty of the state government which was sanctioned the money. The beneficiary was its own inspector! That is why there are many foundation stones laid by VIPs but very few completed projects. The main function of a clever state finance minister was to keep building up convincingly, good projects for the Planning Commission to sanction funds against.

Demonetization has been the second artillery bombardment against black money. The first blast was the abolition of the Planning Commission. Only a few experts realised this; most others are still in a slumber.

MUSLIM LEADERS ARE SCARCE

THE YEAR 2020 brought with it a number of anxieties for Islamic countries. Possibly for the first time Sunni Islam split, not canonically, but politically between Turkey, Pakistan etc. on one side and Saudi Arabia and its allies on the other. The UAE and Bahrain established diplomatic relations with, of all countries, Israel. This, so to say, revolutionary step must have been taken after clearance from the Hejaz or Riyadh. Turkey, which was keen to join the European Union all these years, has lately turned the opposite way towards an Islamic leadership, almost as if President Erdogan wishes to be a Caliph. Incidentally, since the year 1924 the *ummah* has been without one.

Pakistan has become a satellite of China, which incidentally oppresses its Muslim population harshly. Earlier Islamabad was an ally of the USA; what an about-turn! Across Europe, Muslims are no longer welcome. France, the most secular of countries with a president who was elected by defeating

Marie Le Penn the anti-migrant candidate, has had to turn to hounding terrorists. President Emmanuel Macron is having to tell the migrants bluntly that they must either adjust to the French way of life or go back to where they came from. Until recently, Muslim migrants had lived in Europe on almost their own terms, including a demand for eternal graves in Switzerland. Christians reuse the spot of a previous burial after the lapse of some years.

Petroleum has been an economic trump card in the hands of many Islamic countries, apart from West Asia, Indonesia and Nigeria, right through the 20th century. Now the price of crude oil has declined sharply. In the midst of this eco-political crisis, what is absolutely necessary is tall leadership which can show Muslims a direction out of these difficulties. Hitherto, the image of Islam has been one of an expanding torrent. Then came three or four centuries during which the Western world forged ahead from the medieval to modern times and the Muslim world suffered a setback. With the advent of petroleum, again the sun shone on the Islamic destiny.

The turn of the 20th into the 21st century has been not so lucky for them. Nevertheless, to flourish for a thousand years of its total life is remarkable. The question is wither now especially in the face of the internet, the television, the cell phone and all other facets of modernity? Thus far Islam has not been happy or comfortable with modernisation. The religion has been conservative or based on *taqlid* or orthodoxy. *Ijtehad* or reinterpretation has been discouraged over the last ten centuries or so. Confinement of women to the house or to their community, their education limited to the minimum need of women, avoidance of European languages and Western science were together a package which proved to be the secret of Islam's success.

Christianity has permitted continual or frequent reinterpretation and kept pace with modernisation. In fact, it led the wave after wave of change and modernisation although in the process, the Church split into many denominations. However, at this juncture, Islam needs a leader or leaders who can show direction to its people. Going by past record, whenever a Muslim society has thrown up an outstanding *rehnuma* or leader, he has tended to introduce changes unwelcome to the unity and integrity of Islam. Take the latest example of Recep Tayyip Erdogan of Turkey; in his attempt to come into greater prominence, he has split Sunnis for the first time as we have noted above.

Earlier, the stir in the Egypt of King Farouk threw up Colonel Gamel Abdel Nasser whose focus was not merely his own large country but also the whole of Arabia. He even merged Egypt with Syria and created the United Arab Republic (UAR). Nasser paid no attention to the *ummah*, and advocated as well as pushed Arab nationalism, which was to be achieved with the help of socialism. He built the Aswan Dam to irrigate acres and acres of dry Egyptian land. Beyond that, he was unable to do much more probably due to wars with Israel. Nevertheless, Nasser awoke the Arabs to the idea of modernity. Albeit slowly, the Arabs are changing; the current Egyptian ruler Abdel Fattah Saeed Hussein Khalil el-Sisi, also the successor to Nasser, Anwar Sadat and Hosni Mubarak, has rejected the Muslim Brotherhood and called for a reformed Islam. Orthodox countries like the UAE and Bahrain have opened diplomatic relations with Israel. Earlier in Iraq, the late Saddam Hussein was as secular leader as any, so unusual for the *ummah*.

Coming back to Turkey, its great Mustafa Kemal Ataturk took drastic steps to Europeanise his country. Although only three percent of Turkish land area is in Europe, he was convinced that his country's future lay with Europe rather than Asia. In 1924, the Caliphate was abolished and the then Caliph was exiled. What a drastic step! In a matter of three months Ataturk replaced the script of Turkish language from Arabic to Roman alphabets. Even the Quran had begun to be read in the Roman script. He banned the red fez cap and encouraged citizens, including the womenfolk, to wear Western clothes. In short, he turned Turkey upside down. The clergy and the orthodoxy of all other Islamic countries prevented such reforms. Nevertheless, the imprint of the Mustafa Kemal could not have escaped many a Muslim mind.

Any wonder that the clergy and the learned must have, as part of *taqlid*, discouraged the rise of bold leaders. Take our own subcontinent. The pre-Partition *ummah* could not find a leader capable enough to lead them; they, therefore, had to invite Muhammad Ali Jinnah to take over the life-presidentship of the Muslim League. Until this invitation, Jinnah was practising advocacy as King's Counsel in London where at Hampstead he had bought himself a prestigious bungalow. He had been no mass leader until then. He was born an Ismaili Khoja who were called half-Muslim and half-Hindu by the Bombay High Court in its 1861 judgment. Jinnah's grandfather Jinabhai had converted from a Hindu Lohana to Islam. Jinnah himself knew only English and Gujarati and did not speak any Urdu. He, therefore, had to address all meetings in English. It was known that he ate and drank what he liked whether *halal* or *haraam*. Yet he was, 1935 onwards, called Qaid-e-Azam or the great leader.

Jinnah almost overnight became the unchallenged leader of all Muslims in the subcontinent and led them to Partition. Other than him, there were politicians but no real Muslim leader. Sir Syed Ahmed Khan in the 19th century had acquired a stature but he implored the Muslims to learn English and Western science. He founded the Aligarh University for that purpose and asked all Muslims to support British rule. Again, Sir Syed's direction on education was not according to Islamic conservative tradition, apparently a common problem with most leaders of stature. One wonders, therefore, whether in order to sustain the pristine glory and integrity of Islam, the *ummah* have through history tried to discourage the rise of great leaders especially after monarchy became obsolete.

This is not to discount the potential of monarchies to produce leaders. One of the greatest monarchs the Muslim community has produced was the 16th century Mughal emperor of India, Jalaluddin Akbar, who could have become the leader to pull away the community from a structured medieval outlook. Akbar, by his shunning of religious zealotry, acceptance of the validity of other ways of worship, and his particular emphasis on sound governance rather than energetic pursuit of religiosity demonstrated the possibilities of leadership, the legacy of which, had it lasted, would certainly have changed the course of the *ummah* in a fundamental way. Tragically, this was not to be. While Akbar's successors Jahangir and Shah Jahan did not reject Akbar's ways, they were overtaken by Aurangzeb, whose outlook defined by an uncompromising religious zealotry, pushed the community back into the confines of *taqlid* (orthodoxy) and also put paid to any possibility of leadership.

SPORTS WITHOUT GENDER DISCRIMINATION

IS IT not time that an effort should be made to encourage women to advance further in sports? In a game like football it may not be practicable since robust bodily contact often takes place. But what about hockey where girls have made commendable progress? Where one, two or three girl players are somewhat better than the available men for a particular club, university, State or even nationally, should they not be selected? Lately an IPL for women was played in Sharjah and it was a welcome beginning. This step could be followed up by insisting that every men's team should also have at least one woman. Four foreigners are compulsory, several with Test match experience, a few youngsters and so on. Why cannot a woman also be introduced as necessary for every team?

PV Sindhu is our best badminton player at present, probably better than any male shuttler. Why should she be confined to only women's tournaments? Why not give her an opportunity to participate in men's tournaments and become an overall national champion, eventually becoming perhaps an Olympic silver or gold medalist? For long, there have been mixed badminton, tennis and table-tennis teams and tournaments.

This logic should also extend to hockey and cricket. If a girl or girls are better than any male player in their positions, surely they could replace them. Strictly separating men's and women's teams and tournaments is an old mindset based on the women being weaker, less skilled and, therefore, not able to play in the same teams.

Yes, women were much weaker than they are today. In the old days their diet was inferior in all but the wealthy families. Then there were the issues of early marriage and reproduction. Because of a high infant mortality rate, women became even weaker in the days of low technology. Shah Jahan was arguably the wealthiest man in the world in his day. Yet, of his fourteen children he could save only seven—Dara, Shuja, Aurangzeb, Murad, Jahanara, Roshanara and Gauhar Ara Begum. Inevitably, women were considered weak for childbirth took a heavy toll on their bodies.

In olden days, bodily strength was placed at a great premium. Often the king was the strongest man in his court. The weapons were comparatively crude and fighting or defending depended on the man's strength with the weapon serving as an aid. The balance of strength began to shift with the advent of the musket being invented in the 16th century. Its use reduced the importance of the user's personal strength. As more sophisticated guns replaced the musket, they also became lighter in weight enabling women to use them with as much dexterity as men. In the Iraq wars women fought as frontline soldiers. Their relative or presumed weakness did not prove any handicap. If on a battlefield women can prove equal to men, why not also on the tennis or badminton court or the cricket field? Strangely enough, even chess and carom tournaments are played generally by men and women separately; what else is the explanation of this than a sexist bias?

Referring back again to the Iraq wars, we need to make it clear that deploying women on the frontline, whether in the infantry as soldiers or in the cavalry with tanks, or piloting fighter aircraft can create a problem if they are taken prisoner. If the world, not only on the stage but also on the battlefield has travelled so far, why is the world of sport observing what the Islamic world calls *taqlid* or orthodoxy?

It is true that men and women are temperamentally different. The former can look into the future with more perceptiveness, whereas women are more committed to their present. Many of them are also credited with greater intuition. They should be more successful than men at obtaining immediate results.

Of late, this female strength is being repeatedly demonstrated in school board examinations where girl students score higher percentages. Surely, the same strength can be utilised on the sports field.

It is true that the male, whether in the animal or human world, is tempted to dominate, whereas the female is able to function comfortably in a position of subordination. This may be a gift of nature in order to enable the women to carry the responsibilities of child-bearing and breeding. In this regard, nature has been partial; we notice that the male elephant has tusks; the lion has the mane, the peacock the feathers, the cock the red plume. But the will or desire to dominate does not lend itself to team spirit. Stretching this reasoning forward should lead one to conclude that perhaps women have the potential to exude greater team spirit in group sports like hockey or cricket. It is just possible that the readiness to be subordinate might have been cultivated over centuries by women to play the role of the wife to the normally patrician husband.

The tea gardens the world over are an interesting example also of an old mindset now at last changing. The managers, their assistants as well as their subordinate staff are all male; whereas two-thirds of the workers in labour-intensive enterprises have been female. What a paradox! Workers, women; and all managers and supervisors men. Another aspect of these tea gardens is that manufacture of the green leaf into black drinking tea is nothing but cooking without *masala* or any other ingredient. Yet, compared with men, very few women are deployed in the factory. Women are sent out to pluck the green leaves from the bushes and occasionally do other agricultural work. Look at any nook or corner of the world and we find this man-woman paradox.

VETO OR SAYONARA UNO

A PEJORATIVE wisecrack on the UNO is that it has become the 'Useless Non-existent Organization'. For example, in 1999, the then UN Secretary General Kofi Annan suddenly flew into Delhi to 'mediate' in the ongoing Kargil War, only to be politely told by the Vajpayee government to mind his own business and go back. It is reported that this international body has some 100,000 employees from the senior most to the junior most. If the average cost of these men and women is taken to be $50,000, it means an expenditure of five thousand million dollars annually. The organization's other expenses are separate.

The late American columnist Charles Krauthammer had dubbed the UN a "corrupt impostor, undeserving of any American support". Titled "A Table for Tyrants" former Czech President Vaclav Havel wrote an article in *The New York Times* saying that he felt scandalised when he saw the UN Human Rights Council filled with members like Sudan, Zimbabwe,

China and Saudi Arabia, which had no human rights.

Yet, India continues to be an elephantine contributor to the UN peacekeeping contingents, and has sent nearly 200,000 peacekeepers to 44 missions over the years. This is more than the national armed forces of most countries. Indian forces working for the UN have suffered more casualties than any other country's armed forces. Indian policymakers argue that this is being done not for any strategic gain but to serve 'global ideals' like strengthening the world body and international peace and security. The UN did not even condemn communist China's unprovoked aggression against a democratic India in October 1962, leave alone do anything about it. The irony is that the dictatorial, communist China enjoys a permanent seat in the Security Council while India, the world's largest democracy, does not.

The UN also did not support India in its Bangladesh War waged solely to bring relief to East Bengalis who were at the receiving end of Pakistan's genocidal crackdown. The UN passed a resolution making the state of Jammu & Kashmir an internationally disputed territory, despite the clear fact that it was Pakistan that invaded Indian territory in October 1947. The dispute, which has seen four wars and continuing jihadi infiltration and terror attacks, has been geopolitically laid to rest only by India's unilateral abrogation of the controversial Article 370, and not because of the UN. The UN has failed miserably in bringing a terrorist country like Pakistan to heel. It is India that has had to deal with Pakistan on its own. The world body has failed to prevent nuclear proliferation by this rogue terrorist state. In this matter India's boundless naiveté in the Nehruvian era cannot be denied.

The only service the UN arguably performed was to

provide a platform for radical communist elements and a whole generation of dictators and autocrats to portray themselves as leaders and statesman. Most notable in this regard was India's Krishna Menon, whose vitriolic anti-Western rhetoric and fire-spitting speeches in the UN earned him the dubious sobriquet of a "spitting camel". He was so dubbed by the Americans who hated Menon's patronising lecturing but also more seriously earned India a lot of Western ill-will.

The failures of the UNO make an unusually long catalogue beginning with 1948. That year, the Soviet Union blocked Berlin. The only action that prevented the city's surrender was the American airlift of all conceivable supplies in the spirit of *Ich bin ein Berliner* (I am a Berliner), the famous speech of President Kennedy on 26 June 1963 in West Berlin.

In the Korean War (1950-53), the communist North had gone all out to take over the entire peninsula. Again, the UNO could do nothing. It watched Vietnam being bombed more intensively than seen anywhere, anytime, since or before WWII. The UNO, however, remained silent and inactive as ever. In 1956, the Anglo-French invasion allied with Israel against Egypt over the Suez Canal issue; this yet again proved UN incompetence. It failed again the same year when the Soviet Union invaded Hungary. In 1959, the world witnessed the abduction and rape of Tibet by China. In 1968, the international body looked askance at the Prague spring when Soviet tanks rolled into Czechoslovakia. The catalogue of UN acts of omission continues to be legendary.

The idea of an international concert of nations began in the post-Napoleonic period with the primary object of avoiding war. At the start of the First World War, the first schemes for an international organization to prevent future wars began to gain considerable public support, particularly in Britain and the United States. Goldsworthy Lowes Dickinson, a British political scientist, coined the term "League of Nations" in 1914 and drafted a scheme for its organization. Together with Lord Bryce, an Ulster-born academic, he played a leading role in the founding of the group of international pacifists known as the Bryce Group, later the League of Nations Union.

The forerunner of the League of Nations, the Inter-Parliamentary Union (IPU), was formed by the peace activists William Randal Cremer and Frederic Passy in 1889; it is currently still in existence as a body with a focus on the various elected legislative bodies of the world. The IPU was founded with an international scope, with a third of the members of parliaments serving as members of the IPU by 1914. Its aim was to encourage governments to solve international disputes by peaceful means.

The concept of a peaceful community of nations had been proposed as far back as 1795. Immanuel Kant, German metaphysician and philosopher, whose comprehensive and systematic work on the theory of knowledge, ethics, and aesthetics greatly influenced philosophy, in his work *Perpetual Peace: a Philosophical Sketch* outlined the idea of a league of nations to control conflict and promote peace between states. Kant argued for the establishment of a peaceful world community, not in a sense of a global government, but in the hope that each state would declare itself a free-state that respects its citizens and welcomes foreign visitors as fellow rational beings, thus promoting peaceful society worldwide.

International co-operation to promote collective security originated in the Concert of Europe that developed after the Napoleonic Wars in the 19th century in an attempt to maintain the *status quo* between European states and avoid war. This period also saw the development of international law with the first Geneva Convention establishing laws dealing with humanitarian relief during wartime, and the international Hague Convention of 1899 and 1907 governing rules of war and the peaceful settlement of international disputes. As historians William H Harbaugh and Ronald E Powaski point out, Theodore Roosevelt was the first American President to call for an international league. At the acceptance for his Nobel Prize, Roosevelt said: "It would be a masterstroke if those great powers honestly bent on peace would form a League of Peace".

Such an idea should logically have emerged from Europe, whose long history is a record of almost unending wars. At the end of the Great War, the League of Nations came up in the hope of ending the era of war, and giving the West an age of peace. Yet again this idea emerged from an American President, Woodrow Wilson.

But the credibility of the League of Nations was weakened by the fact that the United States never joined the League and the Soviet Union joined late but was soon expelled after invading Finland. Germany withdrew from the League, as did Japan, Italy, Spain and others. The onset of the Second World War showed that the League had failed its primary purpose, which was to prevent any future world war. The League lasted for 26 years; the United Nations (UN) replaced it after the end of the Second World War and inherited several agencies and organizations spawned by the League.

True, the League of Nations did not last long. Yet, credit must go to the League for having spawned the International Court of Justice and the International Labour Organization and other bodies. It is doubtful the UN would leave behind anything memorable except its performance of profligacy. It is high time India told the Security Council to give it a Permanent Seat with veto power. If the Council gives it, well and good, or else, New Delhi should resign from the organisation and thus save itself time, money and honour.

AMBEDKAR AND PARTITION

ACCORDING TO Nehru, Mahatma Gandhi was a Hindu and an Indian, the greatest in many generations, and he was proud of being a Hindu and an Indian (he broadcast this on 14 February 1948). What the Mahatma wrote, said and did is widely known. The track record of Dr BR Ambedkar as a Hindu is not so well-known. His popular image is that of a Dalit leader and a constitutional guru. How much he felt, thought and pleaded for the interests of the Hindus, therefore, deserves recounting.

Babasaheb was one of the few Hindus, if not the only one, who foresaw the consequences of not letting the Muslims have their Dar-al-Islam. He, therefore, openly and in print favoured a partition in almost exact details by 1940. He did this almost on the morrow of the resolution demanding Pakistan which was passed by the Muslim League at its Lahore session on 26 March 1940. He was clear in his view that Partition without an exchange of population was worse than Partition. His reasoning was interesting. To him, dividing the subcontinent was to solve its communal conflict. The Communal Award was given in 1930 when Ramsay MacDonald was the prime minister of Great Britain. The award gave the Muslims what they had demanded at the Round Table Conference. Their weightage as well as their separate electorates were retained; in addition, they were given the statutory majority of seats in the provinces in which they were in majority. The Hindus were also awarded similar privileges.

At that time there were five Muslim-majority provinces and nine Hindu-majority provinces. Since the Hindus had nothing comparable to the Muslim League to lead them, the Congress represented everyone including the Hindus. They did not believe in separate electorates. In fact, they had continually insisted on joint electorates for all communities and had strongly objected to any community being given the majority of seats guaranteed by the Constitution. The privileges which the Muslims celebrated had no meaning for the Congress and its followers. In Dr Ambedkar's perception, in the provinces of Punjab, NWF, Sind, Bengal and Baluchistan, the Muslim governments could treat Hindu minorities as they wished knowing fully well that there was no fear of retaliation in the other provinces because they would have secular governments as distinct from Hindu ministries (as quoted by Dr Ambedkar in his book, *Thoughts on Pakistan)*. The Hindu minorities in the Muslim provinces also insisted on joint electorates although the Communal Award ignored their feelings. It is interesting to recall what Maulana Abul Kalam Azad had to say as president of the Muslim Session held in Calcutta during 1927. In that speech the Maulana declared:

> That by the Lucknow Pact they had sold away their interests. The Delhi proposals of March last opened the door for the first time to the recognition of the real rights of Mussalmans in India. The separate electorates granted by the Pact of 1916 only ensured Muslim representation, but what was vital for the existence of the community was the recognition of its numerical strength. Delhi opened the way to the creation of such a state of affairs as would guarantee to them in the future of India a proper share. Their existing small majority in Bengal and the Punjab was only a census figure, but the Delhi proposals gave them, for the first time five provinces of which no less than three (Sind, the Frontier Province and Baluchistan) contained a real overwhelming Muslim majority. If the Muslims did not recognise this great step they were not fit to live. There would now be nine Hindu provinces against five Muslim provinces, and whatever treatment Hindus accorded in the nine provinces Muslims would accord the same treatment to Hindus in the five provinces. Was not this a great gain? Was not a new weapon gained for the assertion of Muslim rights?
>
> (Quoted from *Thoughts on Pakistan* by BR Ambedkar, Thacker & Company Ltd. Bombay, 1940).

Babasaheb felt that the Communal Award meant that the Hindu minorities would be hostages at the mercy of the five Muslim-majority provincial governments. This, he felt, was a strong enough argument in favour of Partition. Incidentally, the Muslim League at its Lahore Session in March 1940 passed a resolution which amounted to the demand of a separate state called Pakistan. The scheme had been conceived by Choudhry Rahmat Ali in 1933 who advocated a partition. Dr Ambedkar immediately noted that merely the formation of Pakistan would not ensure safety for the Hindus in the Muslim-majority areas. In fact, their condition may worsen because at that time the hostages could at least appeal to the Central Government about their grievances, whereas in Pakistan, there would be no impartial central government to turn to. He recalled that the Hindus in Pakistan could then be given the position of the Armenians under the Turks or the Jews in Nazi Germany.

Babasaheb was perceptive enough to realise that the evil was not Partition but the boundaries of the current provinces which did not reflect or were not consistent with the profile of the Hindu-Muslim population. The boundaries had to be altered; the Punjab and Bengal had to be bifurcated. Even then some Hindus would get left behind in Pakistan and many Muslims would be scattered across Hindustan. All these would then have to be moved in a planned manner so that the Hindus and Sikhs came away to Hindustan and the Muslims moved to Pakistan. This was the gist of Dr Ambedkar's formula. Nevertheless, it is useful to quote him: "That the transfer of minorities is the only lasting remedy for communal peace is beyond doubt. If that is so, there is no reason why Hindus and Muslims should keep on trading in safeguards which have proved so unsafe. That, if small countries with limited resources like Greece, Turkey and Bulgaria were capable of such an understanding, there is no reason to suppose that what they did cannot be accomplished by Indians. After all, the population involved is inconsiderable and it would be the height of folly to give up a sure way to communal peace because some obstacle in it required to be removed".

Babasaheb was convinced that the secret of a happy and successful state lay in homogeneity. That was the lesson taught also by the histories of Turkey, Greece and Bulgaria. Many a constituent of the post-war era has given safeguards for the welfare of the minorities. Their experience, however, showed that these did not save the minorities. Even after safeguards, the same old policy of exterminating the minorities continued. Hence, an exchange of minorities was found to be the only solution. There was another factor which caused Dr Ambedkar a great deal of anxiety. Basing his conclusions on the facts provided in the Simon Commission Report, he found that more than half the soldiers of the then Indian Army were from the North-West Frontier and West Punjab, most of them being Muslim.

Although the British Indian Government justified the profile of recruitment with their theory of martial and non-martial classes, the fact was that during the rebellion of 1857, the people of these areas remained loyal to the British, whereas soldiers recruited by the East India Company from the Indo-Gangetic plains were the ones that actually revolted. This was the view of a Special Army Survey in 1879 which observed that the distinction between martial and non-martial classes was indistinct.

The Khilafat Committee, in its anxiety to safeguard pan-Islamism, had enunciated the principle that the Indian Army should not be used against a Muslim power. The Muslim League had endorsed this principle. In the words of Dr Ambedkar: "Even Theodore Morrison, writing in 1899, was of the opinion that the views held by the Mahomedans (certainly the most aggressive and truculent of the peoples of India) are alone sufficient to prevent the establishment of an independent Indian Government. Were the Afghans to descend from the north upon an autonomous India, the Mahomedans, instead of uniting with the Sikhs and Hindus to repel him, would be drawn by all the ties of kinship and religion to join his flag. The Hindus", he continued, "could find themselves between the devil and the deep sea so far as the defence of India was concerned. If India remained as one whole, what would happen?" The issue might sound remote today but remember, in 1919, the protagonists of the Khilafat movement had actually gone to the extent of inviting the Amir of Afghanistan to invade India.

Even the cost-benefit factor did not escape Babasaheb although he was not a financial expert:

> The Pakistan area, which is the main recruiting ground of the present Indian Army, contributes very little to the central exchequer. The main contribution comes from the provinces of Hindustan. In fact, it is the money contributed by the provinces of Hindustan which enables the Government of India to carry out its activities in the Pakistan provinces. The Pakistan provinces are a drain on the provinces of Hindustan. Not only do they contribute very little to the Central Government but they receive a great deal from the Central Government. The revenue of the Central Government amounts to Rs121 crores. Of this, about Rs52 crores are spent yearly on the army. In what area is this amount spent? Who pays the bulk of this amount of Rs52 crore? The bulk of this amount is spent over the Muslim army drawn from the Pakistan area. It is contributed by the Hindu provinces and is spent on an army from which the Hindus, who pay for it, are excluded! How many Hindus are aware of this tragedy?

IN DEFENCE OF POLITICS AS A CAREER

A LARGE section of the Indian intelligentsia shares the famous writer Nayantara Sahgal's dissatisfaction with the current politics of our country. Her plea for a political counter-culture and an alternative breed of politicians is, however, unrealistic. Her hope that funds, a well-known name, election expertise etc. would become unimportant is misplaced, and the view that "nothing must become one's chief advantage", as she puts it, is evidently impracticable.

The way to overcome the cause of dissatisfaction is to attract to politics more of our citizens who, in turn, would gradually improve the quality of the profession. The answer lies in inducing more of the best citizens to take an interest in the governance of the country, in persuading more and more intelligent, educated persons to face the uncertainties of politics in preference to the security of a steadier vocation. The solution does not lie in replacing the current professionals with a new breed of novices.

By pleading for "a national alternative" and "a new breed" to enter politics, Mrs Sahgal has implied that all or most politicians today belong to "the get-rich-quick cycle". This is not true. One cannot condemn an entire profession because a few of its members are corrupt. "A few" might seem many if one were to go only by newspaper headlines. This is not to blame newspapers, but merely to point out that honest men do not make news; only thieves do. For every house that is burgled in a city, there are ten thousand homes that are not. But in the nature of things, only the burglaries are reported.

Unlike the lawyer, the doctor or the accountant, the politician does not need any professional qualifications. But that does not mean that he does not require professional "qualities". In fact, a politician is called upon to be more versatile than probably any other professional. He must be able to speak, to persuade, to organise, to administer and also to risk the uncertainty and the insecurity of politics. Today a nobody, tomorrow perhaps a minister, and the day after again a nobody. For every politician who becomes a minister there are some fifty others who become nothing. No other calling, except that of a film actor is so uncertain. To expect a new breed to succeed is naïve. The training, qualifications or skills to earn a living in any other profession can hardly be sufficient to be effective in politics.

The diversity of India makes politics even more difficult than in other democratic countries. This has several dimensions. Three-fourths of our people live in the villages. Our village folk are wise and generally vote for the party and the person whom they trust the most. But the person might not be ideal material to be a minister. The variety of our languages makes matters more difficult. The Member of Parliament who knows his language well is often not fluent in any other. He is, therefore, not able to have an adequate say in the affairs of State. By default, therefore, a minority of the legislators are able to dominate the scene. If a few of this minority happen to be irresponsible, they hit the headlines, and from the headlines it looks as if most politicians are corrupt and that all politics is murky.

Politics is competitive, much more so than other vocations. For example, in business a person has only a few competitors. The rest are suppliers, sellers, bankers, auditors, etc. In politics, at one stage or another, almost everyone could be a potential rival. Just as a paanwala does not want another paan shop to open in the neighbourhood, a politician would like to block the entry of another.

Politics is expensive. The expenses are not confined to election, but extend to travel, telephones, correspondence, etc. apart from maintaining oneself and one's family. Life is a lot easier if one is elected. But for every elected legislator there would be anything up to five unsuccessful aspirants. Moreover, most successful politicians too fail to get elected on some occasions. The rising cost of living affects him as much as anyone else. The only difference is that the politician has, most of the time, no regular income.

These are the constraints of politics. They are the reasons that keep many well-meaning people away from the nation's most important profession. It is for the socially-conscious individuals as well as institutions to come forward and support those who are prepared to take the risk of politics but do not have the means to sustain themselves. Incidentally, there are a number of able people in politics who fall by the wayside because at some stage or other, they run out of the means to sustain themselves. It is important to prevent such "sound professionals" from giving up, and lesser men from getting in.

It is most important that families which have several sons and daughters should try to spare at least one member for politics. The others in more secure vocations could support him/her as a matter of family policy. The motivation need not only be patriotic. After all, the family could stand to gain in influence. It would also help to protect the interests of its class.

I have met several patriarchs (who have been critical of the standard of our politics) and asked them how many of their grandchildren they would spare for politics if they were designing the careers of the youngsters. Every time the answer has unfortunately been an emphatic "None". The reasoning might partially have been: "Why should my children bell the cat?" But partly, the explanation lies in our casteist background whereby a profession is chosen more by tradition and less by deliberate choice. Nevertheless, a beginning has to be made at least by the more socially-conscious families.

Otherwise, politics will continue to be what it is. In any case, it is meaningless to exhort inexperienced amateurs to take the field. The answer to "a few" unsatisfactory professionals cannot lie in replacing them with "all" untried amateurs. The answer to an inadequate doctor does not lie in calling a good lawyer!

MARRIAGE AND DIVORCE IN PAKISTAN

IN PAKISTAN, the rule governing marriages is the Muslim Personal Law (The Shariat Application Act 1962) subject to the provisions of the Muslim Family Law Ordinance 1961 and Child Marriage Restraint Act 1929. In these laws there are severe restrictions on polygamous marriages. To quote Section 6 of the ordinance: no man, during the subsistence of an existing marriage, shall, except with the previous permission in writing of the arbitration council, contract another marriage, nor shall any such marriage contracted without such permission be registered under this ordinance. An application for permission under subsection (1) shall be submitted to the chairman in the prescribed manner, together with the prescribed fee, and shall state the reasons for the proposed marriage, and whether the consent of the existing wife or wives has been obtained thereto.

On receipt of the application under section (2), the chairman shall ask the applicant and his existing wife or wives each to nominate a representative, and the arbitration council so constituted may, if satisfied that the proposed marriage is necessary and just, grant the permission applied for. In deciding the application the arbitration council shall record its reasons for the decision. The decision shall be final and not be called in question in any court.

Any man who contracts another marriage without the permission of the arbitration council shall (a) pay immediately the entire amount of the dower or *mehr*, whether prompt or deferred due to the existing wife or wives; (b) on conviction upon complaint be punishable with simple imprisonment which may extend to one year, or with fine which may be five thousand rupees, or with both. Clearly, polygamy, originally permitted by the Shariat has been subjected to restriction. Its crux is that no-objection is essential from the existing wife. Malaysia, which too is predominantly Muslim with the Shariat governing marriage, divorce and succession, has also placed restrictions. A man cannot marry a second wife unless the first wife consents and further, the first wife has to fill in a no-objection form.

In Tunisia, by a legislation enacted in 1956, polygamy was prohibited and made a criminal offence. The Syrian Law of Personal Status of 1953 made the permission for a second marriage dependent on the proved ability of the husband to support a second wife. The Iraqi law of 1959 said there should be some "lawful benefit" involved. In the case of Egypt, a bill which aims at restricting polygamy and the right of the husband unilaterally to repudiate the first wife has been under preparation since 1956. In 1962, on completion of the drafting of the new act, a personal status was announced. The above information is based on *An Introduction to Islamic Law* by Joseph Schacht (Universal Law Publishing Company, Delhi, 1997).

As in Egypt, so in Pakistan there are restrictions on divorce. A free play for the traditional Shariat is not allowed. Any man who wishes to divorce his wife shall, as soon as may be after the pronouncement of *talaq* in any form whatsoever, give the chairman notice in writing of his having done so, and shall supply a copy thereof to the wife. Whoever contravenes these provisions shall be punishable with imprisonment for a term which may extend to one year or with fine which may be Rs 5,000 or both. A *talaq* shall not be effective until the expiration of 90 days from the day on which notice is delivered to the chairman.

Within 30 days of the receipt of the notice, the chairman shall constitute an arbitration council for the purpose of bringing about reconciliation between the parties, and the arbitration council shall take necessary steps to bring about such reconciliation. If the wife be pregnant at the time *talaq* is pronounced, *talaq* shall not be effective until pregnancy ends.

The conservatives amongst the Muslims have repeatedly pronounced they are against a universal civil code. Their contention is that the Shariat is immutable and eternal. That this contention is false is demonstrated by the fact that several Islamic countries have placed restrictions on the practice of pristine Shariat. In India, the most conservative of Muslims accept the Criminal Procedure Code for the punishment of crimes. They do not insist the hand of a Muslim thief be cut off. Similarly, all civil laws, except those relating to marriage, divorce and succession, are common to all citizens.

Justice MC Chagla, in his autobiography *Roses in December*, had occasion to write: "I am horrified to find that in my country, while monogamy has been made the law for the Hindus, Muslims can still indulge in the luxury of polygamy. It is an insult to womanhood; and Muslim women, I know, resent this discrimination between Muslim women and Hindu women," Prof Asaf AA Fyzee in his *Outlines of Muhammadan Law* (OUP, Delhi, 1999), was perspicuous in his observation that greater suffering is engendered by the husband's divorce than by his irresponsible exercise of this right. The tension in the mind of the wife is too great for her to be happy, adding, the law of divorce at least in the Hanafi School was a one-sided engine of oppression.

NATIONAL ADVANTAGES OF SMALL STATES

ONE GREAT enemy of a united India is linguistic chauvinism. Imparting a separate identity to a region or a state and providing a cradle for sub-nationalism can cause the break-up of the country. To the Bharatiya Janata Party, which rules India today, a regional language offers the basis of a rival ideology. The clarion call of language can arouse as much emotion as that of religion. By comparison, the potential of a class struggle waged by the communists or the threat of casteism posed by politicians like the late VP Singh was much less.

Linguistic chauvinism is inimical, especially to a nationalist party like the BJP in another way. Hindutva is an appeal for cooperation amongst economic classes and social castes. Its approach is one of collaboration and not of conflict like that of the communists or of sundry casteist political parties. The former stand for a class struggle; the latter provoke caste conflicts. In this specific aspect, separation based on language is also collaborative among the classes and castes of the particular region. Young men and women in search of a political identity but not trapped by class or caste loyalties would normally follow the BJP. But such youth could get lured away by a more proximate regional movement. There is, therefore, an inherent clash of constituency between the BJP and such a movement.

There is one sure way of eliminating this chauvinism where it has taken root and of pre-empting it where it could grow in the future and that is by encouraging the formation of small states. For example, Telangana and coastal Andhra have been carved out of Andhra Pradesh. The existence of several states speaking the same language automatically dilutes the potential of linguistic chauvinism.

In any case, the BJP's supreme priority is the integrity of India. Prima facie, sub-division may appear a centrifugal move but if considered with an open mind it will prove to be one of the most effective ways of securing India's integrity. Unity through division is a viable paradox. Since India's neighbour Pakistan has undergone a break-up, let us begin with its example. To counter-balance the size of the then East Pakistan, the country's martial law administrator Ayub Khan combined West Punjab, Sind, North-West Frontier Province (NWFP) and Baluchistan into West Pakistan. Instead, had he sub-divided the eastern province into say four, it is a moot point whether Mujibur Rahman could have risen to be its great leader capable of leading Bangladesh to independence. It is entirely possible that Mujib would have remained the leader of only one of the sub-provinces.

It is well to remember here that never in our subcontinental history has one province or state united with another in confronting the Centre. There may be a demand for Sindhu Desh now, but in 1971 not one Sindhi voice was heard in support of East Pakistan. Similarly, when in 1965 Tamil Nadu agitated against the imposition of Hindi, there was complete silence in the rest of South India.

To come to positive examples, both Gujarat and Maharashtra are happier since their separation. The latter continues to flourish while Gujarat has made more economic progress than it would have as a backyard of the old composite Bombay. So, too, is the case with Haryana, which from a backward region twenty years ago has emerged as one of the granaries of India. By being a separate state, it has also remained free from the terroristic disruption of the Punjab.

Economic progress should be easier to achieve in a smaller rather than in a large state. In any case, the progress would be better distributed. The total GNP of a state is no indication of the distribution of prosperity. For example, Gujarat is known to have made industrial progress but most of this is confined to the three districts of Baroda, Bharuch and Surat. The entire Saurashtra-Kutch region continues to lag behind in terms of industrial expansion. The resulting frustration causes disharmony and, if such a region happens to be ethnically distinct, it breeds local chauvinism.

There is nothing sacrosanct about language being the basis of a state. If it were so, Uttar Pradesh, Bihar, Madhya Pradesh and Haryana should be one jumbo state. Similarly, there is no harm in there being three Telugu-speaking or five Marathi-speaking states. On the contrary, several states speaking the same language would take the sting out of linguistic chauvinism which, in turn, would preempt the growth of regional parties, which often end up by voicing separatist sentiments, even if only for their political survival.

The Hindi belt is free of any separatist sentiment. By the

same token its leaders are less sensitive to the fears of the non-Hindi-speaking people. Former UP Chief Minister Mulayam Singh Yadav's ideas about language, propagated when he was in power, are an example. His intentions might have been sincere, with his rhetoric in claiming to speak for all Indian languages and opposing only English. But the message as interpreted by the non-Hindi regions is one of Hindi domination. This does no good for the country's unity.

Except one, our prime ministers have all been from Uttar Pradesh. This might have been on democratic merit but that is not always the way non-Hindi people see it. What strikes them is that Uttar Pradesh has in all 119 MPs (84 of them in Lok Sabha). In sharp contrast, Goa has only three. The die thus appears cast heavily in UP's favour. How can there be a happy federation or a harmonious partnership among such unequal sates?

To elucidate this point, few would have taken any notice if a state like Himachal Pradesh had abolished English. As things are, the size of UP is not proving advantageous to its own people. The state is not considered well-administered nor is the economic development of most of its areas anything to write home about. This is truer of Bihar, so much so that critics contemptuously refer to the cow-belt as the big drag on India's progress.

There are other national advantages of small states. To be the chief minister of a large state is a greater prize than being in the cabinet at the Centre. This would not be so with a small state. As a result, the more ambitious politicians aiming for berths at the Centre would avoid espousing parochial causes.

If we go by the history of bifurcation in India, the sub-division of states should be easy to implement. When composite Bombay and Punjab were bifurcated there was widespread jubilation and little resistance. When Meghalaya,

Nagaland and Mizoram were formed, there was no protest in Assam. Smaller states would be welcomed by the people as well as the local politicians. The only leaders to resent sub-division would be the incumbent chief ministers. Most others are likely to be enthusiastic. For the politicians, smaller states mean more opportunities for the people; it brings about easier access to the centre of local authority. There is no need to travel all the way from Nagpur or Nanded to Bombay to have a grievance redressed. In a small state, the government would also have to be more responsive to the people.

Politically, the promise of small states also helped the BJP to win new following. There were strong demands for Jharkhand, Uttarakhand, or a Gorkhaland, of which Jharkhand and Uttarakhand have become a reality. Demands for other states like Telangana and Vidarbha were dormant for a long time; Telangana has fructified since then. All these constituencies would be grateful to the political party which takes a lead in meeting their demands.

Above all, small states would not be viable nations and, therefore, not aspire to separate from India. A number of the present states are larger than many countries in the world and can threaten to secede as well as survive on their own. On the other hand, small states can safely be granted more subjects and powers to achieve decentralisation, as is the current opinion. To do the same to large states may be fraught with a risk to national unity.

Smaller states would help to achieve six things with one stroke. One, decentralise and make government more responsive to the people. Two, achieve quicker economic progress that is distributed better. Three, by default they make the Centre stronger. Four, they can win new constituencies for nationalist parties. Five, smaller states will weaken inherently anti-national political movements. Six, smaller states secure the integrity of India.

TALE OF TWO TEMPLES

THE FAMOUS Wailing Wall or Western Wall in Jerusalem is the only remnant of the Jewish temple built by King Solomon about 3,000 years ago. It has all through these three millennia remained a holy site for the Jews. Although it was destroyed by the Babylonians in 586 BC, it was rebuilt by King Herod. Unfortunately, this Second Temple was demolished by the Romans in 70 AD. Thereafter, the 35-acre site had to await the building of the Dome of the Rock by Khalifa Umar in 691. Some 25 years later was built the well-known Al Aqsa mosque in the immediate neighbourhood which continues to be looked upon as the third holiest Islamic place after Mecca and Medina.

Incidentally, for a short number of years, in the wake of a Christian victory in one of the crusades, the Dome of the Rock had been converted into a church and named the Holy Domini. The Muslims did not wait too long to reconvert the Dome back into a mosque. The point here is the ease and frequency, and above all lack of embarrassment, with which places of worship have changed hands in Arabia among the Jews, the Christians and the Muslims. This lack of inhibition has also been seen in Europe, be it when the Moors captured Spain from the Christians or when the latter won back their land. Many more places of worship changed hands in Eastern Europe when the Ottoman Turks took over Albania and Bulgaria as well as Bosnia Herzegovina. But the most significant conversion of churches into mosques took place in Turkey. European historians do not hesitate to write about these incidents. In sharp contrast, our scholars have excluded the desecration of temples when writing the history of India.

The Jews have never forgotten or forgiven the loss of their First Temple in Jerusalem but not having control over the holy land, there was nothing they could do about it. Even when the state of Israel was established, the old or the East Jerusalem where the holy sites are located was not in their hands. It was handed over to Jordan under the care of King Abdullah in 1948. During the six-day war of 1967, however, all of Jerusalem was captured by Israel.

The public demand for rebuilding the Jewish temple, however, had to wait till 1990 when an organisation called the Temple Mount Faithful led by Gershon Salomon petitioned the city officials for a permit to lay the cornerstone of a new temple to be called the Third Temple. The Muslims led by Adnan Hussain were panicky. A large number of Muslims gathered in an attempt to try to save the Al Aqsa mosque from the likelihood of demolition. The result was an enormous clash in which many persons were killed.

Incidentally, the Al Aqsa mosque stands exactly next to the Wailing Wall. The battle lines are clearly drawn whereby the

Muslims have to fight to defend their third holiest place against an attempt by the Jews on their holiest site. The Jews consider the Temple to be the national centre of the Jewish nation as well as the location of the divine presence on earth. Even the moderates feel offended by the concerned Wakf trying to introduce material reminiscent of an old mosque below the Al Aqsa merely to show that there was no temple there.

During August 1929, records (as quoted by a historical encyclopaedia of the Arab-Israeli Conflict, Greenwood Press, Connecticut, USA, 1996), show that several hundred Arabs and Jews were killed in what was called the Wailing Wall incident. This was not much before Israel was born but at a time when the British ruled Jerusalem. It bears mention here that the Holy Quran tells the story of Prophet Muhammad's midnight vision of his ascension to meet Allah. This journey took place from Jerusalem which explains why the Muslim sentiments are so attached to AI Aqsa mosque and the Dome of the Rock.

Ram Janmabhoomi is no less dear to the Hindus. This is not to justify the demolition of the Babri edifice in 1992. But it is important to note the colossal embarrassment that was experienced amongst large sections of the Indian intelligentsia, to the extent that to this day regrets and apologies are expressed by one side and charges of communalism are levelled by the other. The worst sufferers are facts and history. To this day, it has not been established as to who were the demolishers of the Babri edifice; whether the domes were broken by one set of people and the walls were brought down by another? Or whether the entire structure was the victim of a single conspiracy?

The only established fact about the whole episode is that the current Ram Lalla temple was built by the Central Government during the Governor's rule by 9 December 1992. The rest of the events are clouded in confusion. Most of the persons present on the day of the incident, also immediately before and after, are around to give their version of what happened. There is a commission of inquiry which is dealing with the matter for several years. If despite all this we cannot get at the truth, when will we ever learn to write true history?

It is amazing that one set of historians has accused another of a communal bias. This set has accused the other of saffronising history whereas the cold fact is that no one has been really interested in recording the truth. The proof of this lies in the fact that there is no book of Indian history which has recorded, at length and in detail, the desecration of even some of the thousands of temples that fell victim to the iconoclastic invaders. Incidentally, there is no shortage of source material. The Archaeological Survey of India, during the days of the British rule, had surveyed the length and breadth of India. One archaeologist alone, namely, Lt Gen Sir Alexander Cunningham has left behind sufficient surveys of architecture in north and central India that have filled 23 hard-bound volumes. These have been published again recently by the ASI.

Then there are the District Gazetteers written at the turn of the 19th and the 20th centuries. These cover almost every district of undivided India. Most of them are diligently written with comprehensive details about the condition of the districts, their buildings, their history, their people and their customs. By themselves, they can be treated as a treasure-house of information if only the followers of history would free themselves of bias.

WHEN TRAVANCORE STOOD FOR TOLERANCE

HARDLY A month passes when someone or the other does not cry out aloud that the evil design of the Sangh parivar is the establishment of a Hindu *rashtra*. A Hindu theocracy is a contradiction in terms, but the argument will be more convincing if it is presented after first facing the loud cry, frontally.

In India, there is one outstanding example of a self-proclaimed Hindu State. A Japanese scholar Koji Kawashima researched and recorded the experience of Travancore between 1858 and 1936 in his book, *Missionaries and a Hindu State* (OUP; 1998). The study was funded by two Japanese foundations called Yoshida and Morita and supervised by a British professor, David Arnold. It can, therefore, be relied upon as an impartial, objective work on an Indian State. The following excerpt from the book helps to describe Travancore's state Hinduism as well as how the non-Hindi citizens were treated:

> In India, the kingly duties have been called *rajadharma*, which can be defined as the obligation of the ruler to protect dharma or to secure peace, prosperity, justice and order in the kingdom. Of these duties, protection of the gods and their temples was perhaps the most important. As a servant of Sri Padmanabha, the Maharaja of Travancore observed a number of rituals, most of which were started by Martanda Varma in the mid-eighteenth century. Travancore had a large number of non-Hindus, particularly Syrian Christians. In 1875, Christians formed about 20 percent of the population, and Muslims six percent. These different religions seem to have coexisted and largely integrated into the Hindu state in pre-modern Travancore. One of the principal reasons for this coexistence was a semi-official state policy of religious tolerance.

Regarding this, Lieutenants Ward and Conner, who surveyed Travancore and Cochin from 1816 to 1820, stated that Christianity was fully acknowledged by the chief authorities in those states and, whether from their justice or indifference, does not appear to have been exposed to persecution. Knowles, an LMS missionary, stated in 1898 that the Travancore state was conspicuous by its tolerance of non-Hindu religions. In fact, Hindu kings gave the Syrians privileges and honours that distinguished them as a high caste. The Syrians themselves attempted to have the support of the king when there was a dispute over ecclesiastical power within their church. Also, as Leslie Brown, an American historian has pointed out, Syrian Christians joined in many Hindu festivals.

Evidently, the Hindu state of Travancore did not discriminate against the followers of other faiths. The overriding evidence of this is the present population profile of Kerala, a large part of which had belonged to Travancore. Incidentally, the other major states of what is now called Kerala were Cochin and Malabar; both were ruled by Hindu monarchs. As far as religious tolerance was concerned, they were similar to Travancore. In fact, all the three were so tolerant that they freely allowed change of religion. Today, 20 percent of Keralites are Christian and a similar percentage Muslim. Why is, therefore, a periodical outcry against the Sangh parivar's reported wish to establish a Hindu *rashtra*? Assuming this is true and successful, no one has any need to fear going by the prototype as represented by Travancore.

The implication is that the Hindu ethos has no tangible model of the state. It is undeniable that Ram was looked upon as an ideal king. The *Mahabharata* discusses the three prime duties of a king, namely, protecting the borders of the state, ensuring justice, law and order for the people and selecting a competent successor to the throne.

Dhritarashtra does instruct Yudhishthira about the ideal judicial and legal set-up for the kingdom. He also speaks of a strict penal system and insists on the right kind of punishment for crimes. Also addressing Yudhishthira, Bhishma explains the duties of a king, especially in the context of the economy as well as defence. Sri Krishna's wisdom is wide-ranging as well as fascinating. The *Bhagavad Gita* is a theory of life which is valid eternally. His guidance through the epic has a great deal to teach about strategy as well as practice for life as well as the battlefield. Yet, there is no theory on the state and certainly not anything on a Hindu polity. Evidently, even in those ancient times, worship was kept far away from the conduct of the state. Otherwise, somewhere or the other we should be able to come across the theory of a Hindu state.

Kautilya's *Arthashastra* is far more comprehensive about how a kingdom should be governed. Nevertheless, even if one were to build the model of a state on the basis of the details, there would be nothing Hindu about a Kautilyan policy. To the best of my knowledge, there is no mention of either worship or religion in *Arthashastra*. The model would be strictly secular in the original European sense of the state being separate from the church.

Coming to recent times, Mahatma Gandhi did talk about Ram Rajya whose model he did not construct on paper. Nevertheless, it was his idea of an ideal state. One essential sentence from Gandhi needs to be quoted here: "By Ram Raj, I do not mean Hindu Raj. By Ram Raj, I mean Divine Raj and the Kingdom of God. For me, Ram and Rahim are the same deity". Even then, when a non-Hindu hears the word Ram, he takes it for granted that the concept is that of a Hindu state.

GLOBALISATION WITH SWADESHI

THE TAKEOVER by the World Trade Organization (WTO) of the superintendence of international commerce from GATT (General Agreement Tariffs and Trade) signalled the inexorable march to globalisation. It is difficult to think of a single country where every trade or every individual is not for the breaking down of barriers as are dictated by comprehensive globalisation. There are reservations, if not also objections, to some factor or the other. Nevertheless, it is clear that most countries have, willy-nilly, got drawn into the tide directed by the WTO. China is one of the few sizeable nations that have recently acquired a presence in the organisation.

An essential point is that every economy wishes to export as much as possible and earn foreign exchange. It, therefore, desires every other country to have low import duties. On the other hand, most countries would prefer fewer imports. We in India know this very well. This is the contradiction which has been masterfully exploited by the proponents of globalisation.

At the economic stage at which India is, there are large sectors in the economy which view the prospects of free imports with consternation. Even those on the fringes of business realise that the tide of globalisation can drown a great deal of Indian entrepreneurship.

For several weeks there were reports that the automobile industry is doing well as a result of sales being far higher than the previous years. This is a healthy economic symptom, but it is also a reminder that most of the automotive industry is already in foreign hands. As late as 1991, it was all indigenous except for the 51 percent share held by the Japanese in Maruti.

In a matter of eight years, the country lost control over a major unit. The inexorable logic of the trend is that the manufacturing sector will, before long, be owned by foreigners. For Indian entrepreneurs, the playing fields would largely be confined to the tertiary and the leisure or the other sectors like services, tourism, transport etc.

As the larger Indian entrepreneur squeezes into his shrinking playing field, he is likely to push out the smaller Indian businessman. And it is this smaller Indian entrepreneur, whether retailer, trader or manufacturer, who is in many ways the pillar of our commerce. One of the strengths of the Indian ethos has been that a significant number of its citizens know many a trade like the back of their hands. If this pillar is shaken, where will the big businesses rise from in future? After all, the present large businesses are already under pressure, if not also declining. In any case, to bank on a few families producing entrepreneurs forever is not a wise practice.

It is not impossible that, unless a way is found, the indigenous businessman, in twenty-five years' time, would be a shopkeeper, a petrol pump owner, a stockist or a distributor.

Not many of his ilk are likely to be anywhere near the commanding heights of the Indian economy. What then is the way out? The answer lies in a medium or an individual sector. A company, whether proprietorship, partnership, private or a public limited one, in this sector could have an equity or capital not exceeding, say Rs 10 crore. All shareholders must be individuals, whether Indian or foreign. No company, trust, or even an HUF should be allowed to hold any share. This is to ensure that no large corporation can ever come to control or influence such an enterprise. A company in this sector should be exempted from the levy of central indirect taxes like excise duty. In any case, any fiscal expert would confirm that collecting taxes from larger units is much easier and more economical. This exemption would give it the advantage that a smaller entrepreneur should have when pitted against a large corporation, whether multinational or Indian. This would also offset the disadvantage that a smaller unit carries due to its smaller scale.

Simultaneously, another problem of our economy can be tackled provided this individual sector is made free from the Industrial Disputes Act so that its units are able to go for upgrading. They should be free to hire employees at market rates, and be free to dispense with their services if and when the orders happen to shrink. For instance, this would greatly help the garment exporters. For then the manufacturers would be able to have large factories and control quality and thus seek large orders. At present, the tendency among Indian garment manufactures is to avoid big challenges and hand out on a job-work basis to smaller suppliers, whereas in China there are factories where thousands of tailors stitch clothes on the same factory floor.

For the protection of the employee, it would be best if perhaps 25 percent of his wage was given to him with his monthly salary or fortnightly wage. This 25 percent should be in the form of a bank draft payable exactly five years hence. This would be in lieu of provident fund, gratuity, medical benefits etc. On termination of employment, the worker would then be free to quickly seek an alternative job rather than get bogged down in trying to realise his past dues and benefit money.

This medium or individual sector would ensure entrepreneurial opportunity for smaller and the medium businessmen who, in turn, would make it possible for Indian entrepreneurship to keep thriving and throw up individuals or families that can build large corporations. The medium sector is not merely to protect anyone. It is also to ensure a fertile soil for the future growth of Indian-owned businesses.

LET PUBLIC SECTOR GO PUBLIC

THE PUBLIC sector is a millstone around the neck of the Indian economy. Until it is substantively disbanded, government capital will remain locked up and more funds will be wasted every year to keep many of its sick units alive. The sector is inefficient and does not contribute enough to the nation's economy. Even the profitable units are inefficient and collect surpluses by monopoly pricing. In sum, the public sector is holding down the country's economic growth and is a major cause of inflation.

The origin of the public sector assuming the commanding heights of the economy lies in a mistaken interpretation of socialism. The essence of socialism is equal opportunity for all citizens. One classical definition is "from each according to his ability, to each according to his opportunity". How does the ownership of enterprise by government achieve equal opportunity? It only replaces individual entrepreneurs with the government, which means not socialism but "state capitalism".

The justification of large investment in industry and trade by the government was that private entrepreneurs could not raise capital on a large scale, and that private capital might not find the returns from infrastructural projects remunerative enough to make investments. Some of these arguments might have been valid at the time they were given, but over the years they have largely worn out.

The motivation behind the proliferation was the human urge for 'empire-building' and the advantage that patronage over vast projects gives. Whether the politicians or bureaucrats, many fell prey to this urge. Otherwise, how does one explain the establishment of trading corporations? Or why should the distribution of diesel and petrol be in the public sector?

This background is not to waste time and space on the past but merely to recount that the justification of the public sector was limited even at the start. Now, of course, the sector has proved to be a failure and a big burden on the economy. A look at what has happened in the Soviet Union and Eastern Europe shows how disastrous a command economy can be. It is, therefore, time we begin to completely disband the Indian public sector, however long and difficult the process.

To begin with, the profit-making non-core corporations should offer 74% of their shares to the public. The shares should be valued on current worth and full premium charged to the investing public. The issues should be managed commercially as in the case of private sector companies. The sale proceeds would begin to reduce the enormous debts and deficits the governments of India have run up. When all the accounts are searched and totalled, the figures would run into lacs of crores of rupees. The statistics given at budget time or piecemeal at other times conceal rather than reveal the true situation.

Incidentally, there are quite a few government enterprises with public shareholding. The State Bank of India, Indo-Burma Petroleum, Balmer Lawrie and Andrew Yule are some examples. And all these are showing profits.

Apart from releasing thousands of crores of rupees, the public sector going public would have other advantages. The managements would become more autonomous and, at the same time, more alert about their performance. With the general public investing in their companies, the managements would be more alive to performance. The tendency to be satisfied more by following the correct "procedure" and less by performing profitably should show a distinct change. With the shares quoted at the stock exchanges and the press comparing the performance of the various companies should induce them to be result-oriented. Over a period of time each company would develop its own commercial culture and thus become more and more businesslike.

Managerial 'motivation' and performance 'monitoring' are two missing links in the public sector. This is not to say that the managers are not motivated or that the undertakings are devoid of monitoring. It is merely to emphasise that motivation and monitoring, of the kind essential to industrial enterprises are not inherent in the structure of the public sector. This absence is an important explanation for the uneven performance. The calibre of the managers and the quality of the plants are not, as a whole, inferior to their counterparts in the modern, private sector companies. Yet, the results of many units are unsatisfactory.

Managerial 'motivation' is a complex phenomenon. It is not to be confused with the simple factor of 'incentive', whether monetary or promotional. In any case, we are discussing the phenomenon more at the level of chief executives and Board members and less in the context of departmental managers. Motivation needs a comprehensive system which offers the manager the scope to fulfill himself. It calls for an environment wherein he can give his best; whereas 'incentive' is merely a tangible bait. At the level of the chief executive 'incentive' has little value. In any case, when a person chooses to be a manager rather than become an entrepreneur he is reconciled to the limits of pay and perks. When he takes over as chief executive, he knows he has reached a plateau beyond which there are no greater peaks. At most, he can look forward to heading a larger corporation.

To be able to give his best, a manager needs essentially two things. He must have the freedom or rather the free hand to outdo his own performance of the previous year as well as to outclass other comparable managers. To put any policy hindrance in the way of such a free hand is to demotivate the manager. This freedom is not enough unless he has the opportunity to display his skills and to seek applause. The manager at his best, therefore, is rather like an athlete, who, all the time, wants to run faster than his peers and, at the same time, break his own previous record. And having done that, he expects the crowd to applaud him.

A manager's gallery consists of his company's Board of Directors, its shareholders, its bankers, its customers, its suppliers and dealers, its competitors and so on. Then there are the stock exchanges, the chambers of commerce, the newspapers and the magazines. The public sector manager tends to miss out on most of this gallery. His board is loaded with officials who are trained more about procedure than profits. The shareholder is most often the President of India represented by officials. Not many of the undertakings have competitors. The question of stock exchanges and chambers of commerce does not arise, and only bold managers go to the press; the rest are better advised to avoid the possibility of controversy.

The public sector manager is like an athlete with a track but no stadium and no gallery. This is not to say that every manager knows what he is missing but that is small consolation. When the men of Bharat Heavy Electricals play hockey, they play the game exactly as it should be played in all its details and dimensions. Why then should they manage their company differently from what is commercially necessary? Ownership, whether public, private or mixed, has little to do with how industry needs to be managed.

Ownership only determines to whom the manager is accountable. An owner can change the game and its rules only at his cost. In hockey he would lose by goals, in industry he would lose profits.

With so many members of the public looking for their dividends, the companies would have to become result-oriented. The shares would be bought and sold on the stock exchanges. They would be quoted and their prices would be compared with the shares of the other companies. Investment experts would analyse them while newspapers and magazines would comment on the performance. In due course, the companies could become members of chambers of commerce, whether new or the existing ones. With the need to be result-oriented, the managers would have to be given a free hand in running the companies. They would thus find their much-needed motivation.

Shareholding by the public and the need to be result-oriented would also be the beginning of active monitoring.

Performance monitoring is another missing link in the public sector. But, interest by the individual shareholders, however active, could only have a limited effect. Similarly, there are limits to which the stock exchanges and the press could serve as monitoring agents. The government would still remain the major shareholder with 26 percent and have the responsibility for monitoring. The question is how should the government do so meaningfully?

A government department is an administrative unit. Its officials are trained to administer departments but not to manage companies. The emphasis of an administrator is on correct procedure whereas the challenge of a management is to produce results. It is unfair to expect someone who has not managed a company to monitor its performance. It is, therefore, essential to get managers to be monitors.

It is equally necessary that, to be effective, the monitors should have a stake in the companies they are watching. For, unless the shoe pinches one is apt to be casual if not indifferent. With government ownership, there cannot be a personal stake but there certainly can be a professional stake. Why not get the public sector chief executives to monitor one another?

What if the President of India sold his shares of every public-sector unit to the other public-sector undertakings? There could be cross-holding of shares. If necessary, the financial institutions (including the insurance corporation and the nationalised banks) could be asked to lend a hand in holding the shares.

In order to ensure that the shareholding is well spread, no company should hold more than 2 percent in any single unit. This would result in ten to fifteen or more government companies being represented at the shareholders' meeting of every public-sector unit. With crores of rupees of his company invested in the shares of another unit, the chief executive is bound to take interest in that unit. He would watch the unit's working and expect dividends. If the unit cannot pay dividends, his company would have invested money without getting a return. This in turn would affect the results of his company. And he has to face his shareholders. In the end, as it were, most chief executives could thus be monitoring the performance of every unit.

We would have set managers to monitor managers! Professionals would be watching their peers with full knowledge of what is possible and what is not. Bureaucrats would be spared the responsibility of checking on companies which they have not managed. And the President of India would have, over a period, encashed his investment without losing complete control over the public sector.

SYMPATHY FOR SRI LANKAN TEA

IF SRI Lankan Prime Minister Mahinda Rajapaksa wished to increase trade with India, his stress would have been on the bilateral since SAARC had turned dysfunctional. A few odd misunderstandings between the two countries needed to be cleared. Though the fault was not India's, its image in Asia was of an unfriendly big brother. It, therefore, needed Sri Lankan friendship for diplomatic reasons. Sri Lanka's unique location makes it, unlike Nepal, geopolitically free from domestic compulsions. There has never been a substantive cause of animosity between India and Sri Lanka. The Tamil tea garden workers were, until the 1960s, an irritant. Though they had been taken there by plantation owners to grow, tend, pick and manufacture tea, their numbers were a cause for concern. The Shastri-Sirimavo agreement of 1965 resolved the problem.

Jaffna's Tamils are Sri Lanka's own. They have been there since time immemorial. They are certainly no newer than the Sinhalas who form the majority of the island's population. If only the late Prime Minister Rajiv Gandhi had been advised sensibly, the Indian peacekeeping force need not have gone there. As things stand, the small neighbour may harbour suspicions about the bigger country or be circumspect about the fact that India has a large Tamil State with whom the Jaffna people have scattered associations.

If the Tamils are mostly Shaivite, the Sinhalas are mainly Buddhist. They had joined the *sangha* of Lord Buddha at the special persuasion of Emperor Ashoka who sent his daughter Sanghamitra all the way to Sri Lanka. The political definition of a Hindu, whether by Veer Sarvarkar or anyone else includes the Buddhist; in fact, anyone whose faith took birth in India. For the Sangh Parivar and its allies, therefore, Sri Lanka is a Hindu country. This is all the more reason for India to build a lasting friendship.

Tea can play a role in demonstrating India's generosity of spirit. We produce much more tea than Sri Lanka does, but the two countries export similar quantities. The island country's own population is so small that most of its produce has to be exported. There was a time until around thirty years ago when foreign exchange earnings from tea mattered a great deal to India. Tea and jute used to compete for the top earner's position. In the bargain, several of our ministries used to vie with Colombo as a rival.

We have not quite outgrown that complex. Today, tea does not figure in the honours' list of exchange earners. In fact, the industry should cease to chase exports, It should let importers pick what they want of Indian tea spontaneously and leave the export rivalries to small countries like Sri Lanka and Kenya to whom earnings from the beverage are a matter of economic life and death; a third of their GDP contrasted with a quarter to half percent of India's!

Having taken tea seriously, the Sri Lankan effort at internationally marketing the produce has been incomparably superior to ours. Its exporters have explored every nook and corner of the tea-drinking world. If only there was free trade between the two countries, a significant quantity of CTC tea could find its way into Sri Lankan tea bags. For our neighbour, this means more exports without having to invest in converting its factories to CTC manufacture.

India should abolish rivalry and expand bilateral trade by lifting customs barriers and giving aid, if necessary, to nearby friendly countries. Sri Lanka offers an opportunity for India to establish a reputation as neither a bully nor a big brother but a generous neighbour.

VITALISING THE PUBLIC SECTOR

MOST OF our public sector units are administered and not managed. There is a vital difference between administration and management. The former is connected with doing the right thing as per rules dictated by equity. Administration is procedure-bound. It is required to maintain a desirable status quo and is not meant for producing anything. However, running an industry calls for more. Management begins with a target and a plan for reaching it. Then should follow a budget of what the plan would cost and a time-table for monitoring the progress. It ends with either the attainment of the target or with an acceptable explanation for falling short. It is a result-oriented exercise wherein rules are only means to an end.

All the districts of the country can be administered more of less with the same procedure. But an industry or an enterprise needs to be managed and that too distinctly, according to the nature of its business. Unlike administration, management cannot be uniform in all the units. Producing steel needs an approach different from insuring lives, so does running an airline from distributing petroleum, or marketing wrist watches from banking money. Then again, these enterprises operate under different conditions. Some like Indian Airlines are monopolies. Others like the general insurance corporations have competitors in the public sector, while yet others like the banks or Air-India have to compete with both the public and the private sector whether Indian or foreign.

First Step

As a first step to reorganise in response to these realities, the President of India should cease to own the public sector corporations. The shares of every corporation should be sold to other public sector companies. Take the Steel Authority of India Limited (SAIL), for example. Its shares might be taken over by say, the LIC, the Unit Trust, the nationalised banks, the general insurance companies, Hindustan Machine Tools, State Trading Corporation and so on. No unit would hold more than five percent shares of any one company so that every enterprise would have a fair number of shareholders. SAIL, in turn, could hold the shares of a number of these same corporations. With this change, every enterprise would cease to be the appendix of a department of the Government of India. To enable each company to develop its own distinctive culture, the Bureau of Public Enterprises should be made to minimise the monolithic influence. Subject to essential guidelines on matters like audit rules and emoluments of senior employees, the Bureau should stay off the companies.

The change would increase and not reduce the checks over the public sector units. At every shareholders' meeting there would be present twenty to twenty-five chief executives of other corporations. They would be concerned with the dividend and the return on their investment. They would, therefore, spontaneously keep a watch on the performance of each other's companies. And their watch would be professional and, therefore, expected to be knowledgeable and constructive. They should bring to bear on the situation inter-corporation comparisons which are the key to motivating business managers. Inadequate motivation is a major cause of the uneven performance of the public sector. A typical government officer or a bureaucrat looks for authority at work and security of job. The business manager is different. He gets into his element when he is given the opportunity to demonstrate his professional excellence. A true manager is rather like an athlete in search of a perpetual tournament where he can go on winning fame. A comparison between his performance and that of his peers urges him to greater and greater effort.

An essential prerequisite to getting the best out of a business manager is to give him a free hand. Name a target, agree on a plan, demand a budget, prescribe the rules, but thereafter leave him to his devices for a year at a time. Do not burden him with non-business constraints. Government control over pricing of products is a frequent constraint on the public sector. To peg prices at artificially low levels is demoralising for any business enterprise. Defeatism grips the whole company. The managers ask; what is the sense in working hard if the Government is going to cheat us out of the fruits of our corporate effort? This would be an all-pervading, even if silent question on the lips of most in the enterprise. Price control could become the excuse for every inefficiency in the unit. A sense of hopelessness that it doesn't matter what we do, we will make a loss, could overtake all managers. Negligence, embezzlement, every kind of corruption then tends to get swept under the carpet of price control. No business can deliver the goods under such conditions.

If prices of socially-essential goods have to be controlled, let them be controlled but with the help of a separate organisation. Let there be a separate body which buys at a price fair to the manufacturer and which sells at a lower price necessary for overriding social reasons. The loss should be made up by the national exchequer with the help of a subsidy so that everyone would know the cost of the subsidy without diluting the efficiency of production.

Business and welfare do not match well. A number of public sector units are either overstaffed or wrongly staffed or both. There are units which may be rightly staffed for the technology currently followed by them. But the technology of some of these units is outdated and it cannot be changed and updated for fear that some workers may become redundant. Which manager can bell such a controversial cat? And so he lumps it with obsolete techniques at incalculable cost to the national economy.

Job Security

There is a way of providing job security without burdening an industry with too many workers of the wrong kind or with an obsolete technology. An enterprise could have a panel to which employees, whether workers or executives, who are surplus, might be deputed. The Bureau of Public Enterprises should keep in touch with all such panels. Whenever vacancies occur in the public sector, the first preference should be given to those on the panels. As a compensation for uncertainty, all employees on the panels might be paid an allowance, say 10 percent of their gross wages, over and above their full normal dues. This scheme would give a free hand to public sector managements to shape their companies on business lines and gear them towards peak efficiency. The cost of paying for them would be insignificant compared with the gain in efficiency. In business, the cost of a correctly-placed employee does not need to be counted. His output is much greater than his wage. On the other hand, the cost of an ill-adjusted or an unwanted employee is incalculable. It is not just his wage but all the damage he does by working inefficiently and causing disaffection among his colleagues that proves costly.

Our public sector units have capable chief executives and competent managers. Most of them are better educated than their counterparts in the private sector. Most of the enterprises are well-conceived. The plants, the machines and the materials are sound. The ownership is desirable and enlightened while in the private sector the ownership is often diffused and the managers do not always know the owners. Except in the family-managed concerns, this is often the case. Yet, the best of these companies performs phenomenally well. In other words, everything is more or less right with our public sector except the environment. It is at present expected to do business under a system where the rules are bureaucratic and where the aims are those of a public utility.

WANTED ANOTHER SECTOR IN INDUSTRY

INDIA'S INDUSTRIAL growth has been slow and of late has been stagnating. The primary cause is the Central Government's faulty industrial policy. There is plenty of demand for goods, raw materials are by and large available, machinery is not difficult to get and there is no shortage of technocrats. Where then is the bottleneck?

Admittedly, our large complex society does not lend itself to the free uninhibited policies that have been successful in small unitary nations like Korea, Singapore or Taiwan. Our solution must, therefore, be a consensus that not only answers the economic needs of industry but also allows for the socio-political constraints of India.

Before mooting such a policy consensus it should be useful to recapitulate first the social realities and then their political corollaries which cannot be ignored by any industrial policy in India. The mass poverty and the wide material disparities between the poor and the rich breed a distrust of the business class. This distrust is not confined to the poor but extends to many who are well-to-do but who are not in business or industry. In other words, there is a pervading suspicion of the entrepreneur's intentions. There is yet another distrust almost in-built in the country and that is of the foreigner. Probably because of our colonial past, the average Indian tends to assume that when a foreign entrepreneur or a multinational comes to India, he or it is likely to profiteer and carry away large surpluses overseas. Whether either of these suspicions is justified or not is of limited significance to the policymaker. He has to allow for them because they are reflected in the views of many of our legislators.

There is another side to entrepreneurs which no contemporary industrial policy can afford to ignore. And that is that modern industrial technology is not easy to obtain except from entrepreneurs, whether they are the so-called Indian monopolists or the multinationals. It should be remembered that technology is not merely a technique of production but also a method of management. Even communist China is beginning to acknowledge this by shopping for collaborators from the capitalist world. Any policy which excludes the monopolists or the multinationals is therefore likely to be a non-starter.

Yet another fact of the Indian economy is the scarcity of entrepreneurs in relation to the size of the country and the scale of growth necessary.

Whatever be the technological postulates, the country's political sensibilities must be fully respected, especially if a policy is to be enduring. Industrialisation needs gestation time and, therefore, a policy which will be consistent for at least a couple of decades is essential. No matter how pragmatic a policy, if it is threatened with frequent changes it cannot yield results. In order to ensure such consistency, the policy should be the product of a national consensus. It should not only satisfy all shades of political opinion in the party ruling at the Centre but also carry most of the ideological biases represented by the parties in Opposition.

Yet another pre-condition for a successful policy is the implicit support of the public servants.

TAXES: WHY SHOULD PEOPLE PAY?

THE ESCALATING inflation is a matter of grave concern to all those Indians who have, more or less, a fixed income. Emoluments seldom rise in step with the prices of goods and services. Nevertheless, those employed in the organised sector are somewhat protected. Those in the unorganised sector face an uncertain future. If electricians, plumbers or carpenters happen to be in short supply, they may be in a position to raise their charges ahead of inflation. But perhaps a potter, a tailor or a dhobi may not enjoy the same privilege due to competition.

Unskilled or semi-skilled workers face impoverishment because a rising population supplies more and more of them. Except in the event of war, inflation means irresponsible spending by the government.

Contrast this phenomenon with what William Pitt the Younger did two centuries ago. Pitt, who became Prime Minister at the age of twenty-four, was widely derided as a schoolboy. He was three years out of Pembroke College, Cambridge, when he became premier. While in the course of his 22-year career as prime minister he acquired many a feather in his cap, his most original contribution to finance was the setting up of a Sinking Fund for his country.

This concept was sharply opposite of deficit financing. The fund was to be built with the help of surplus budget. Plans were to eventually make it so large that the interest earned by it would suffice to pay for the British Government. There would then be no need for taxation. In the initial years, the fund accumulation gathered momentum with one surplus budget after another. The achievement would appear extraordinary if we recall that Pitt began with a national debt of a staggering 250 million pounds largely caused by England having to combat the American Revolution.

Pitt soon wiped out the deficit, and in 1786 introduced the principle of an annual surplus of at least a million pounds. The Sinking Fund would have kept growing but for the raging Napoleonic war which first broke out in 1793 and, thereafter, consumed more and more of the national budget. As a result, the Tory government had, for the first time, to print notes as a means of increasing money supply a La deficit financing.

In the budget of 2006-2007, Finance Minister P Chidambaram allocated Rs l, 72,728 crore as plan expenditure. Of this enormous sum, only Rs 28,996 crore was earmarked for capital expenditure, namely development or adding new assets to the national economy. The balance, Rs l,43,762 crore, was declared for revenue expenses. The argument was that assets that had been created in the past needed to be maintained. The revenue portion of the planning expenditure was for the sake of maintenance. Incidentally, the total Central Budget was Rs 5,63,99l crore.

For instance, if a 50-km long road was built in Bihar ten years ago, it needed repairs and maintenance every year. True, but was that development? Even if one fell in line with the Planning Commission's thinking, one might ask how the Yojana Bhawan knew whether the revenue money sanctioned was spent on sand, stone chips and coal tar, or it was spent on paying salaries to the State PWD staff.

The Yojana Bhawan had no evidence whatsoever whether the road was built at all. The implementation was supposed to be a state matter and, therefore, the responsibility of the government at Patna which meant that the planners sat back in their armchairs and sanctioned money. The chairman would get himself photographed once every year with every chief minister and, thereafter, forget about the money he had sanctioned.

On the other hand, nothing by way of a developmental scheme could be undertaken by a State, or for that matter the Centre, without sanction of the Planning Commission. Even a museum costing 10 crore could not be built unless the Yojana Bhawan gave its clearance. Imagine, therefore, the enormous authority that the Planning Commission enjoyed without any accountability. In the Union Budget for 2006-2007, it had allocated Rs 1, 72,728 crore or 31 percent of the budget. The substantive use that was being made of the Commission was neither planning nor development. It was to keep the Central grip over state governments.

The favourite State could be allocated more while those run by the opposition parties could be kept on a shoe-string budget. The old proverb, "He who pays the piper calls the tune", was practised on a grand scale by Yojana Bhawan. A blatant example was the grant of Rs3,250 crore to Bihar soon after Mr Lalu Prasad Yadav joined the central ministry. West

Bengal appeared to have been the next beneficiary of central largesse. Or else, what would have led Mr Montek Singh Ahluwalia, the Deputy Chairman of Planning Commission, to visit Kolkata post-haste after his appointment?

So long as that type of planning continued, there was no hope that the waste of money would cease or that the deficits would shrink. At the same time, it was essential that no money be wasted and that development begins to yield returns. If this was an acceptable proposition, the Planning Commission should have been converted into a Development Ministry, which could go before Parliament and raise a cess exclusively meant for expenditure on development projects.

The Ministry would also be free to raise loans from the market, whether at home or abroad. Whatever it collected every year by way of cess and loans could be matched rupee for rupee by a grant from the Reserve Bank of India which, in turn, could raise the money by deficit financing. Having to approach Parliament for the cess would bring a certain amount of accountability.

More importantly, having to service loans would make the Ministry's work even more accountable. Unless projects yield results in a reasonable time, the interest on the loans cannot be paid. There should be no other reason for deficit financing except perhaps in the event of war. The revenue expenditure of the States as well as the Centre should be met from current revenues.

CHECK MINORITIES COMMISSION OR CLOSE ARCHAEOLOGICAL SURVEY

IT IS not widely realised that just one 19th century archaeologist, Lt Gen Sir Alexander Cunningham has left behind records sufficient to fill 23 hardbound volumes recently published by the Archaeological Survey of India (ASI). These records are a minuscule part of the survey treasure available with the ASI. Hardly any of this literature is referred to in the books of Indian history. Yet, the self-styled secular historians have the audacity to protest that there is no need to fill the gaps. Any attempt to rectify matters is alleged to be saffronisation.

The ASI seems to have been misguided since Independence. It has not only been neglected but its work has been perverted by vested interests. Thus, one of the fountains of historical information has been deliberately stifled.

Had the two constables of the Reserve Police not been asleep on 29 June 2000, I would have been denied the privilege of seeing an archaeological treasure of my homeland. For about twenty minutes, I was able to walk around the Rudra Mahalaya complex at Siddhpur in the Mehsana district of Gujarat. I was also able to take a minute off to have the darshan of a shivling in the premises. I could not go much further because one of the constables woke up and politely told me to leave the precinct as he had strict instructions from the government not to allow anyone to enter the Rudra Mahalaya.

Siddhpur is to departed mothers what Gaya is for dead fathers. In fact, it is called Matrigaya where a Hindu can offer *shraddh* to the soul of his mother. Bindu Sarovar is where the ceremony is performed. Equally dear is Siddhpur to Gujaratis, as the city is named after Gujarat's most famous monarch who ruled in medieval times. After he attained *siddhi* or success as the most powerful king of northwest India, if not the whole subcontinent, he attained the title of Siddhraj. His name was Jaisinh Solanki (1094 to 1143 AD).

On the intervention of the National Minorities Commission since 1983, the Archaeological Survey of India has been prevented from carrying out any excavations in or around the Rudra Mahalaya complex where once existed the tallest temple in Gujarat. From its top were available glimpses of Patan, the capital of the ancient kings of Gujarat, some 25 kms away. From the top it was believed that some temple *mashaals* in Ahmedabad (when the capital was shifted there by Ahmed Shah in the 15th century) were also visible. Even today, the ruins demonstrate the beauty of the sculptures, though many human faces have been mutilated.

The tablet displayed at the spot by the Archaeological Survey says the following:

This is the grandest and the most impressive conception of a temple dedicated to Shiva associated with Siddhraj who ruled in the 12th century, though tradition accords its construction to Mularaj during the 10th century AD.

Only a few fragments of the mighty shrine now survive. With its adjacent shrines, part of which were converted into the Jama Masjid later in the Mughal period, it must have formed a grand composition dedicated to the Ekadasha Rudras.

The Jama Masjid mentioned above is a modest affair. Its gate is so small that not more than two persons can enter at the same time. On its top are two minarets less than three feet tall. As one crosses the gate, there are four small temple sancti, one on the left and three on the right. It is clear that the sanctum had been walled up and converted into a prayer space. Beyond this is the square tank which was also used by those who came for *ibadat*. Yet beyond stand a few handsome pillars and carvings that have survived from ancient times.

According to a neighbour, no prayers take place except for the odd Hindu who drops in for darshan of the only surviving *shivling* in one of the four sanctums. The brick walls of the other three have also been removed although there are only platforms without the idols.

The National Minorities Commission influenced the government, both at Delhi and at Gandhinagar, into freezing the excavation work that was begun by the Archaeological Survey in 1979. The details are available across 38 pages in the Commission's own fourth annual report dated 1983. The improvement of the environments of the masjid were first conceived in 1959 in response to a complaint repeatedly made by the local Muslims that the Archaeological Survey had been neglecting the repair and upkeep of the masjid. Yet, after 1983, the Commission has not only ensured that the work he frozen but also that all the excavations recently made should be covered up. And this has been done despite what came out—a stone *nandi* bull in a mutilated condition. The rest of the relics were covered up. These included a *shivling* from the northern side of the complex and an idol carving from the southern cubicle. The details are given on pages 135 and 136 of the Commission's fourth annual report. Evidently, the list proved so embarrassing to the Muslims that their leaders were anxious to bury the discoveries.

According to the report, Began Aysha, an MLA, played a leading part in this cover-up operation. Shri KT Satarawala, the then adviser to the Governor of Gujarat, also played a yeoman's role by providing a detailed report on the subject. That the Muslim appellants were able to push the Archaeological Survey about is best quoted from the fourth annual report itself:

> Shri AS Qureshi, Advocate for the (Muslim) Trustees issued a notice dated February 6, 1980, to the Superintendent, Archaeological Department, asking the Department to build the compound walls as per the compromise and to cover up the temple remains. The Superintendent, Archaeological Department explained in person the importance of the discoveries made and the need for revision of compromise in the interest of preserving the precious cultural heritages of the country.
>
> As Shri Qureshi wanted to visit the site along with Superintendent, Archaeological Department, he went to Siddhpur on March 8, 1980. At first, he agreed to the preservation but later he insisted on closing the trenches in his very presence that day. The Superintendent, Archaeological Department, ordered closure of the trenches and construction of compound wall and both the works were started in his presence.

The west and the north are at present streets with common people living in small houses. On the eastern side there is space with no vested interest. That leaves the southern side of the current part of the complex. There is the Dawoodi masjid and attached to it is a fairly large area which houses the masjid complex including the quarters of the people who work in the institution. Dawoodi Bohras are the most influential community of Siddhpur and, evidently, their leadership is worried about the consequences of any excavation. If we go back to what is written on the tablet displayed by the Archaeological Survey quoted above, there is mention of eleven shrines for Ekadash Rudras. At the very most, four of the shrines are visible today. Where are the remaining seven? Evidently, the fear is that they are below the complex that today houses the Dawoodi masjid.

Should the work of the Archaeological Survey be allowed to be halted by the intervention of the National Minorities Commission? Should a national commission work at the behest of a narrow local vested interest? Or, should not the government rein in the Commission from undertaking such obstructionist activity? If there is legitimacy to such activity, would it not be logical that the Archaeological Survey of India be wound up? This, of course, would imply that we have lost interest in a search for our civilizational heritage. But certainly Lord George Nathaniel Curzon, who founded the Archaeological Survey and redeemed the Taj Mahal, would turn in his grave. After all, he had bought from Cairo, with his own money, two lamps that hang near the sepulchres of Shah Jahan and Mumtaz Mahal.

FUNDAMENTALISM ISN'T BARBARISM

THE DASTARDLY throwing of acid on young girls by militants in Kashmir is surely worse than anything that the Taliban are reported to have done. In the fundamentalist view, being ruthlessly strict might be desirable but surely religious discipline should not apply to children. The Taliban are undoubtedly fundamentalist but that does not add up to their being barbaric. True, compelling Hindus in Afghanistan to wear yellow in order not to be mistaken for Muslim is understandably upsetting, as was the earlier Bamiyan episode in which two 6th century monumental statues of Buddha were destroyed. Nevertheless, there is a difference in being obscurantist and in being uncivilised.

To be made to wear yellow is to be declared as a protected citizen or a *dhimmi*, i.e., someone who is not *momin* but a non-believer who has paid his taxes or *jizya*. This tradition originates in the Holy Quran. A non-Muslim subject of a Muslim state belonging to the Jewish, Christian, or another faith, who, for the payment of a poll or capitation tax, enjoys security of his person and property in a Mohammedan country. To adhere to this tradition is to be faithful to the book. In the Judaic ethos, humanity has invariably been classified into at least two sections, the Christians and the heathens, the *momins* and the *kafirs*. The Taliban are being forthright. The Christians are theologically discriminatory about the heathens although in practice they are less candid about what they believe.

Nevertheless, the evangelists continue to proselytise in many parts of the world. His Holiness the Pope, as recently as the year 2000, declared that there was a harvest of souls to be reaped in Asia. It also needs to be remembered that Christian theology did not provide a formal option to the non-believers whereas the Muslims did by offering to recognise a *dhimmi* status for those prepared to pay *jizya*. The status incidentally carried preconditions such as wearing yellow for the Jews and blue for the Christians. Hindus and others came to be offered the status after the conquest of Hindustan. In contrast to the Judaic or Semitic ethos, the Hindu universe conceptually includes all living beings; humans, animals, birds, reptiles et al.

In fact the Taliban are absolute fundamentalists. As is known, a fundamentalist is one who follows and quotes the holy scriptures in any argument whatsoever. The expression "fundamentalist" was first used in the US soon after World War 1, when Charles Darwin's theory of evolution had begun to be taught. Since it contradicted the teachings of the Holy Bible as to how the world came into being, it offended many Christians. The orthodox amongst them quoted line and verse from the Bible as to how God created the universe over six days and rested on the seventh.

The evolutionist liberals called these orthodox Christians

"fundamentalists". The Taliban in the 21st century epitomise an example of fundamentalism. But such absolute faith, however ill-suited to this century, is not barbarism. It is fanatical, zealous, dogmatic, bigoted, yes; but barbaric, no. Such a condemnation would amount to running down one of the world's great religions, namely Islam.

The Bamiyan episode and the iconoclasm it personified made many Hindus weep. But to someone devoted to another philosophy, such destruction must have appeared legitimate, if not an act of piety. The cornerstone of the Semitic ethos has been monotheism or an absolute faith in one god. In the eyes of a Jew, a Christian or a Muslim, even a suggestion or a hint of an alternative deity is unthinkable. This explains his apparent revulsion at the sight of an idol or an image of worship.

Prophet Muhammad was so scrupulous that he did not distinguish between an idol for worship and an ordinary statue. He did not want to take any chance by allowing any discretion to his followers. He, therefore, did not permit the use of imagery whether of animal, man or of god. Portraits, statues, paintings, etc. were forbidden or *haraam,* lest they attracted devotion in competition to Allah. This commandment applied not only for the future but the Prophet Muhammad saw danger even in the past, in all the idols that existed.

Merely because today such a distinction seems incongruous or hateful does not amount to its being barbaric. What the Taliban is doing to the women of Afghanistan also appears abhorrent. Yet it was Islam that in the seventh century rescued the Arabian womenfolk from the degradation of their being mere chattels. Prior to Islam, a woman formed an integral part of the estate of her husband or father. Hence the frequent unions between stepson and mother-in-law were forbidden by

Islam under the name of *Nikahu'l-Maqt*, or 'odious marriages', as stated in the *Dictionary of Islam*, 1885, compiled by Thomas Patrick Hughes. The fault of the Taliban is that they are imposing principles of conduct that were framed 1400 years ago in Arabia. They should have changed since but they insist on being consistent with the fundamentals of pristine Islam.

HINDU-MUSLIM SCHISM

THE HINDU-Muslim divide is as old as the invasion of India by the Afghans, Turks and Iranians. The pre-Islamic invaders must have been equally ruthless but they did not retain their separate identity. They adapted themselves into the local social milieu, which was Hindu. The Muslims, on the other hand, not only retained their Islamic identity but also made efforts to convert the local populace. Those who did not convert became victims of the poll tax or *jizya* and were looked upon as *dhimmis* or protected citizens. Moreover, many a conqueror tried to establish a *Dar-al-Islam* in his kingdom and rule according to the Sharia as brought out by Professor S Abid Hussain in his book *The National Culture of India* published by the National Book Trust, 1972.

It was, therefore, not surprising that in their hearts the Hindus had grown to hate the Muslims. At the same time, by and large, the Muslims did not hate but certainly harboured contempt for the Hindus. This mutual attitude reflects the

Hindu-Muslim equation right through the centuries until the British began to assume power in India. Until then, the Muslim was the ruler and the Hindu the subject across large tracts of the country. No doubt, there was a phase when the Marathas gained influence but their domination was neither permanent nor widespread enough to correct the Hindu-Muslim imbalance. This imbalance explains why there is no record of communal riots until after 1858 when the British crown directly assumed governance. How could there be a riot between the ruler and his slaves? Riots can only take place when there is a semblance of balance.

The advent of the British signalled the defeat of those princes who were in power. Much more of India was ruled by nawabs than by rajas. The Mughal emperor was the titular head of the country; even the Marathas acknowledged him as such. The defeat was complete and formal when the rebellion of 1857 failed. As the British became rulers, the Muslims as well as the Hindus became the subjects. Thus, equality was established for the first time. For the Hindus, it was a great relief that they had ceased to be either *dhimmis* or *jizya* payers. The British were impartial rulers who acted as umpires between the two communities.

These are the facts. Yet, the myth of divide and rule was created. Evidently, neither British scholars nor rulers were able to nip it in the bud. Surely, they could not have relished being accused of such an unscrupulous policy, which indicates that there is yet another myth that our history has been written with bias only because the British did so while they ruled the country. They must have intervened and favoured angles that served their own interests. At the same time, the bias was not all theirs. Our own scholars and politicians also played their part in twisting historical conclusions. And herein, the greater responsibility must lie with anti-Hindu Hindus, for the simple reason that Muslim leaders were forthright.

Maulana Muhammad Ali, who was the principal lieutenant of Gandhi in his Satyagraha campaign in 1920-21, refused to join him in the second campaign in 1930. At a meeting of the All India Muslim Conference at Bombay in April 1930, attended by over 20,000 Muslims, he bluntly stated: "We refuse to join Mr Gandhi because his movement is not a movement for the complete independence of India but for making the seventy millions of Indian Musalmans dependents of the Hindu Mahasabha". He made no secret of the fact that the Muslims, as a whole, were guided by pan-Islamism. He told the members of the Round Table Conference that Islam was not confined to India. He said, "I belong to two circles of equal size but which are not concentric. One is India and the other is the Muslim world...We are not nationalists but super nationalists". In his address as Congress President in 1923 he had reminded the audience that extraterritorial sympathies are part of the quintessence of Islam (*History of the Freedom Movement in India*, Volume III by RC Mukhopadhyay, 1977).

As is well-known, Muhammad Ali and his brother Shaukat Ali were followers of Mahatma Gandhi when he led the Khilafat movement to protect the throne of the Sultan of Turkey and the Khilafat of all Sunni Muslims in the world. They lost all interest in Gandhi when in 1924, Kemal Ataturk, the Turkish general, exiled the sultan and abolished the Khilafat.

There are a few highlights from the *Lal Ishtihar* or the Red Pamphlet written by one Ibrahim Khan of Mymensingh district in East Bengal early in the 20th century (Volume 2 by RC Majumdar, 1975):

> Musalmans arise, awake! Do not read in the same schools with Hindus. Do not buy anything from a Hindu shop. Do not touch any article manufactured by Hindu hands. Do not give any employment to a Hindu. Do not accept any degrading office under a Hindu. You are ignorant, but if you acquire knowledge you can at once send all Hindus to Jehannum (hell). You form the majority of the population of this province. Among the cultivators also you form the majority. It is agriculture that is the source of wealth. The Hindu has no wealth of his own and has made himself rich only by despoiling you or your wealth. If you become sufficiently enlightened, then the Hindu will starve.
>
> Hindus are very selfish. As the progress of Mahomedans is inimical to the self-aggrandisement of Hindus, the latter will always oppose Mahomedan progress for their selfish ends. Be united in boycotting Hindus. What dire mischief have they not done to us? They have robbed us of honour and wealth. They have deprived us of our daily bread. And now they are going to deprive us of our very life.

Evidently, these are not the ravings of a normal person. Yet, the depth of emotion reflects the deep divide between the two communities. British manipulation to divide Indians could not add up to such venom, nor any administration responsible for law and order would possibly encourage this. This does not mean that the British did not take tactical advantage of the differences in order to sustain their rule. The point is that the divide was old and deep and the British were the beneficiaries.

Decades have gone by since the British left the subcontinent, yet the tension between the two communities abounds; between India and Pakistan, between India and Bangladesh and between the Hindu and Muslim brethren within the country. Why? Because, as Prof S Abid Hussain has lucidly explained, unlike other Indian communities and most Asian people who honour as sacred the values of patriotism and loyalty to the state, Muslims are unanimous in rejecting what Western nations explicitly believe in i.e. the priority of country or state over religion (*The National Culture of India*, National Book Trust, 1972).

The Hindu confirmation of these Muslim contentions is given by Nirad C Chaudhuri in his *Autobiography of an Unknown Indian* (published by MacMillan & Company Ltd, London, 1951) thus:

> When I see the gigantic discord of these days I am not surprised, because we as children held the tiny mustard seed in our hands and sowed it very diligently. In fact, this conflict was implicit in the very unfolding of our history, and could hardly be avoided. Heaven preserve me from dishonesty so general among Indians of attributing this conflict to British rule, however much the foreign rulers might have profited by it. Indeed, they would have been excusable only as gods, and not as man the political animal, had they made no use of the weapon so assiduously manufactured by us, and by us also put into their hands. But even then they did not make use of it to the extent they might easily have done. This, I know, is a very controversial thesis, but I think it can be easily proved if we do not turn a blind eye to the facts of our history.

A British view of the schism between the two communities is provided by Sir Percival Griffiths ICS, in his book *The British Impact on India* (Macdonald & Company Limited, London, 1952): "India stood sharply divided between Hindus and Muslims. The feelings between them were such what could be expected, since one community had been dominant and the other subject, and often, though not always, oppressed".

Much has been made of the separate electorates as an attempt by the British to divide and rule. Here is what Sir Percival had to say:

> Indian politicians have bitterly reproached Britain for introducing the principle of communal electorates in the Morley-Minto reforms. In reality, there was no practical alternative. If semi-parliamentary bodies such as the Morley-Minto Councils were to mean anything at all, it was essential that all communities should be genuinely represented in them. The gulf between the Hindus and the Muslims at that time was wide, and nobody with experience of modern India will doubt that under any system of joint electorates the Hindus would have secured the return of non-representative Muslims. The philosopher might deplore the fact the Hindus and Muslims thought of themselves as separate peoples, but the statesman had to accept it. The fears of the Muslims were real and deep-seated. When the Congress leaders some years later formed a temporary alliance with the Muslims, they too had to recognise those fears; perhaps the greatest justification of the British establishment of communal electorates lies in the fact that they were recognised in 1916 by the Lucknow Pact.

WHY MUSLIMS DREAD EXCAVATION?

WHY DID the pro-Babri masjid lobbies not welcome the expediting of the case? They had been consistently opposing the Government of India's plea to the Supreme Court to hear the case at the earliest. They had even more vehemently resisted the Allahabad High Court order that the truth should be discovered through excavation. Why? All these years these very proponents of the Babri masjid had again and again sworn that they would abide by a court verdict, whatever it be. Their stand was that the Ram Janmabhoomi is a property dispute. What better than a judicial verdict? Justice expedited is justice delivered. Justice delayed is justice denied.

Behind this contradiction is the fear of excavation being accepted as the mechanism for discovering the truth about temples. Looking at this syndrome from the Muslim point of view, one would be filled with sympathy. Nearly all the pre-Lodi period masjids and dargahs were direct conversions of Hindu temples. The buildings continued to stand as they were.

Either the heads of human or animal figurines were cut off or their faces were disfigured. Thereafter, *mehrabs* were fitted to indicate the direction of *namaz* and *mimbars* were built for the imams to stand and read their khutbahs (sermons).

As JD Beglar, the Assistant-Director of the Archaeological Survey of India (ASI), in his report for 1871-72, wrote: "It is only after the Mughal conquest that Muhammadan architecture begins to be beautiful". Before that the Islamic approach to architecture was barbarous. According to the readings of the invaders, "their religions demanded the suppression of aesthetic feelings". Nevertheless, with the advent of the Lodis who preceded the Mughals, direct conversion of temples to mosques was much reduced and the technique of recycling was developed. According to it, the old temple was brought down to the ground level. The foundation was used to rebuild a newly-designed masjid or dargah. The rubble comprising of well-polished columns, slabs and stones was extensively used. Care was taken to ensure that the original carvings, whether of faces, bells or flowers were concealed by being turned either into the floor or the walls. Only the reverse smooth side of the stone was exposed.

The Muslim dread of excavation is an old one. It dates back to 1871 when Beglar had suggested the examination of aspects of the Qutab Minar as well as the tomb of Sultan Ghari in Delhi. To quote him: "I am most sanguine that, on a careful examination of the inner courtyard, after stripping the irregular layer of stones which Muhammadan barbarism has spread, traces will be discovered of some central shrine".

After Maulana Abul Kalam Azad became the Education Minister in 1947, the ASI preferred to avoid controversies. A series of legislations were passed in 1951. Their thrust was the regulation of archaeological excavations. The implied policy was not to excavate freely but to protect what had been discovered. The culmination of this freeze policy was the Places of Worship (Special Provisions) Act, 1991. It declared that the character of any place of worship, as it existed on 15 August 1947, could not be changed. Ironically, when Vicerory Curzon consolidated the ASI in 1904, he went out of his way to stress that it was our duty towards posterity to make sure that we discovered and preserved India's heritage.

An outstanding example of the ASI's preference for concealing rather than excavating heritage is the Rudra-Mahalaya complex at Siddhpur in Gujarat. At the repeated exhortations of the local Muslims, the ASI decided to beautify the surroundings of the Jama Masjid. As the digging began for laying a garden in the surroundings, several artefacts including a Nandi bull were recovered. These discoveries embarrassed the local Muslims so much that they took the help of the Gujarat Government, the Ahmedabad High Court as well as the active intervention of the National Minorities Commission to stop further excavation. Their advocate himself supervised the burial of the fresh artefacts. The fourth annual report of the commission covers the details of this episode.

The Bijamandal at Vidisha, 40 km from Bhopal, is another example of embarrassment at the discovery of artefacts. Some fresh ones were discovered on a monsoon night of 1991 when a wall on the apron of the edifice collapsed. The local ASI officer was helped by the District Collector in the effort to salvage the new discovery. In a short time, both these officers were transferred by the government.

The Muslim dread of excavation is particularly understandable if one remembers that there are some 3,000 temples turned mosques or dargahs in the country. If Hindu extremists insisted on excavation of all these buildings, imagine the scale of conflict. As a corollary, the floors and the walls could also face the axe.

ZAKIR HUSSAIN'S COUNSEL FOR MUSLIMS

"OUR MISGUIDED brothers in Pakistan do not realise that if Muslims in Pakistan can wage a war against Hindus in Kashmir, why should not Hindus, sooner or later, retaliate against Muslims in India"? This was a part of the memorandum submitted by Dr Zakir Hussain and three other Muslim leaders to Dr Frank P Graham, UN Representative in Kashmir, on 14 August 1951. That was seventy years ago. It is indeed a pity that India has never thought of taking the help of its Muslim citizens, most of whom can be the country's useful allies against Pakistani misdemeanour.

There is no doubt a problem. About the only viable Muslim leadership in the country is ecclesiastical. The luminaries who are not maulvis do not have sufficient following. Addressing Muslim citizens through the *ulema* has its limitations. The substantive interest of the masses lies in a peaceful life where the individual and his family can try and prosper; educate their children and so on. On the other hand, the thrust of the *ulema* would be to protect and promote the influence of Islam. The leaders of India, therefore, should find a channel of informing and seeking cooperation of our Muslim brethren directly.

The memorandum was also signed by Sir Sultan Ahmed, Sir Mohammed Usman, both former members of the Viceroy's Council. The signatories included the Nawab of Chhatari, Chief Justice of Allahabad, Sir Iqbal Ahmad, Sir Fazal Rahimtoola, AK Khwaja, TM Zarif, BH Zaidi and Hafiz Rehman, the last two were MPs. Their submission also said: "If the Hindus are not welcome in Pakistan, how can we, in all fairness, expect Muslims to be welcomed in India? Such a policy must inevitably, as the past has already shown, result in the uprooting of Muslims in this country and their migration to Pakistan, whereas it became clear last year, they are no longer welcome lest their influx should destroy Pakistan's economy".

There was also a background to this fear. Several Muslim League leaders had repeatedly emphasised in the years preceding Partition that when the country was divided, there must be an exchange of population.

MA Jinnah, Khan Iftekhar Hussain Khan of Mamdot and Pir Ilahi Bux of Sind repeatedly asked for a complete exchange of Hindu-Muslim population as an integral corollary of Partition. The statements of these gentlemen were reported by the *Dawn* on different dates in 1946, and have been quoted by Justice Gopal Das Khosla who had been commissioned by the Government of India to lead a fact-finding mission.

This explains why the memorandum states that: "Pakistan is incapable of providing room and livelihood to the 40 million Muslims of India, should they migrate to Pakistan. Yet its policy and action, if not changed soon, may well produce the result which it dreads. Pakistan claims Kashmir, first, on the ground of the majority of the State's people being Muslims and second, on the ground of the State being essential to its economy and defence. To achieve its objective, it has been threatening to launch jihad against Kashmir in India". Is it not remarkable that jihad today was threatened more than seventy years ago? What we call a proxy war today was declared long years ago.

The advice implicit in what Dr Hussain wrote needs to be conveyed to the masses, especially the Muslims. This is not easy because our masses do not always read newspapers. The *khutbah* read by the Imam just before the Friday prayers is about the most effective medium for the Muslims. But here there are two problems. One is that there are very few mosques in India where the womenfolk are admitted. This makes the *khutbah* communication confined to the men who attend the Friday prayers. The others including womenfolk have to depend on hearsay.

The other great problem is that the Imam is a part of the community of the ulema. He, therefore, conveys what is consistent with the ecclesiastical policy whose central thrust is the preservation of pristine Islam and not necessarily the welfare of the masses. Take for example the advice given by the ulema to the masses especially after the Rebellion of 1857. It was to shun English education and avoid western science. Later in the century, Sir Syed Ahmad Khan made yeoman's efforts to persuade the Muslim intelligentsia into ignoring this advice and taking to Western studies. As part of his efforts, he founded what is now called the Aligarh Muslim University. He insisted that the head of the teaching institution should be British so that English and Science got the emphasis that was needed.

Sir Syed did his best but he was only partly successful. The result has been the widespread Muslim complaint that they are backward and, therefore, they need special consideration by employers. The policy, in the view of the ulemas, helped their religion although an objective perception would be that Islam has a powerful faith. Prophet Muhammad's message should run deep into the Muslim heart regardless of ecclesiastical intervention.

While concluding the memorandum, Dr Zakir Hussain and his friends wrote: "We should, therefore, like to impress upon you with all the emphasis at our command that Pakistan's policy towards Kashmir is fraught with the gravest peril to the 40 million Muslims of India".

THE JIHADI ORIGIN OF THE 1857 REVOLT

JIHAD (FIGHT against enemies of Islam) has indeed enjoyed a colourful history. Throughout the 19th century, inspired by the Wahabis, the Muslims waged jihad against the British in India. In his book *The Indian Muslims* (George Allen and Unwin, London, 1967), M Mujeeb states that in the first years of the 19th century, Shah Abdul Aziz, a scholar of Hadith, issued fatwas declaring India to be Dar-al-Harb (house of war). He complained that in the city of Delhi, Imran-ul-Muslimeen wielded no authority, while the decrees of the Christian leaders were obeyed without fear. From Delhi to Calcutta the Christians were in complete control. Haji Shariatullah of Bengal declared that India had become *dar-al-harb*, and the *jumma* and Id prayers should not be performed publicly. He stated that it was a basic doctrine of Islam to carry jihad against *kafirs* and to insult them was to honour and praise the Prophet.

Mujeeb goes on to quote Maulana Abul Kalam Azad, to say that in 1913 this was reason enough for jihad to follow inevitably, and no one could be a Muslim or even a believer in one God unless he undertook jihad. In line with the Wahabi thinking, Sayyid Ahmad Barelvi worked hard to establish a new Islamic state in the North-West Frontier area and assumed for himself the title of Imam and Commander of the Faithful (*The Oxford History of Islam*; New York; 2000; page 528). In 1821, he appointed two *khalifas* or representatives, based in Patna. This was confirmed by Sir William Hunter in his well-known work *The Indian Musalmans*, originally published in 1871 and reprinted by Indological Book House, Varanasi, in 1969. Incidentally, Sir William wrote this book as an apologia to a question mooted by Lord Mayo, the then Viceroy of India. The question was: "Are the Indian Musalmans bound by their religion to rebel against the Queen?" The answer to the question evidently was 'yes'. As Hunter put it, "the jihad of Sayyid Ahmad Shahid against the British was carried on intermittently for over twenty years".

As early as 1831, most of the region north and east of Calcutta lay at the mercy of jihadis led by Titu Miyan, alias Nisar Ali. The three districts of 24 Parganas, Nadia and Faridpur especially were in the hands of Miyan's followers. As Sir William has described, on 6 November 1831, some 500 of the jihadis raided many a village, murdered the temple priest, slaughtered cows, defiled the temple with their blood and hung the carcasses before the idol; this was their way of proclaiming the extinction of English rule and the re-establishment of Mohammadan power. It was after a prolonged action that the English militia was able to defeat this detachment of jihadis and kill Titu Miyan. Nevertheless, the followers of Imam, Sayyid Ahmad and Titu Miyan, continued to appeal to every Musalman to join the holy war against the English infidels.

The inspiration behind this jihad was one Abdul Wahab who grew up in Damascus during the 18th century. He preached that the true believer must be loyal to jihad. Being a loyal servant of the British Company, Sir William called the Wahabi ringleaders traitors. However, not sentenced to death, they were subjected to lengthy trials and those convicted were transported for life, presumably to the Andamans. However, Indians couldn't have agreed with Sir William about the Wahabis being traitors, rather, they must have looked upon the British as the aliens. It should also be noted that the Hindus were mostly at the receiving end of the jihadi brutalities and, as a result, were against the movement. The introduction of the secular penal code and the appointment of judges who could dispense justice according to it also made a great difference, whereby the Qazis also became redundant.

The senior ulema felt that with the abolition of the Qazis, a *dar-al-Islam* in India had become a *dar-al-Harb*. As Hunter put it, "Had the Musalmans been wise, they would have perceived the change, and accepted their fate". But an ancient conquering race could not divest itself of the traditions of its nobler days. How could the Muslim tolerate a system which gave no advantage to him over the Hindu whom he hated as an idolater and despised as servile? With the advent of the British, several other privileges he enjoyed during the rule of his co-religionists dwindled. He ceased to be the obvious candidate for army officership. In Hunter's words: "The Musalman monopoly of rural oppression ceased. Due to the newly-introduced 30 years resumption laws, the landlords, most of whom were Muslim, became insecure. After Lord Cornwallis' Permanent Land Settlement, the majority of the new zamindars happened to be Hindu, which proved to be a deathly blow to Muslim prosperity".

The hurt pride of the Muslims fuelled by the Quranic ideology of jihad and fanned by his economic displacement sustained the holy war. It spilled over into the cataclysm of 1857, which was triggered off by the soldiers of the company, but which, in effect, was the final military tussle between the Indian princes and the English. The princes, mainly Muslim, including a few Hindu rajas, joined forces hoping to recover their fiefdoms. As Hunter recorded: "During the mutiny of 1857, the first act of a Musalman rebel, when he proclaimed the Delhi Rule in a city, was to call on some Muhammadan local saint for a fatwa declaring holy war against the English". To quote RC Majumdar, "The news of the mutiny of sepoys at Mirat was followed immediately by the capture of Delhi and the declaration of Bahadur Shah as the Emperor of Hindustan".

CONDITIONED MINDSET

HARDLY A week passes without our rulers talking of economic growth, whether six, eight or ten percent. They, however, do not appreciate the utilisation of assets. Everyone needs some rest every day and also requires a periodical break, perhaps once a week; but neither the rest nor the break needs to be at night or on a Sunday. Yet, the greater part of the country's urban economy comes to a grinding halt on that day. Many offices, including those of the Government of India, are closed on Saturdays as well.

The logic of Sunday is that it is a "day of the Lord". To this has been added Saturday as the Sabbath. How many Indians are either Christian or Jewish? Why not, therefore, let some of the others work on the weekends? Two out of seven days is nearly 29 percent of the time. If, therefore, the offices and other establishments remain open all seven days, they could help to employ up to 29 percent more people.

Not a month passes without the governments making a

noise about the need to increase employment opportunities. Understandably so in a society which suffers from almost universal under-employment.

The other glaring irony is the under-utilisation of physical assets including roads, buildings, offices, vehicles et al. To illustrate, there are several million cases pending in the law courts across the country. Justice is much delayed and, therefore, often denied. Yet, no court sits beyond one session or shift.

The Delhi High Court sits, after discounting holidays, for 210 sessions in the year. There are 25 judges or courts which means a total of 5,250 sessions. If instead there were 75 judges who, in turn, conducted three sets of sittings or shifts round the clock, there would be 15,750 sessions. Justice would then move three times faster, apart from providing employment to three times the number of people, lawyers and others.

Crores of rupees that have been invested in the High Court building would then be utilised and would bring a higher return on the society's investment. On the one hand, it is contended that India is a poor, capital-short country. On the other, we waste the capital assets we have.

There are few people in Delhi who do not complain about traffic jams. Yet, over the weekends, the roads of Delhi are underutilised. The Indian society is a prisoner of outdated mindsets; for example, no passenger minds an international flight taking off say at two am, but domestic flights do not start until about six am.

Even worse is the fixation over school timings. Respectable schools should begin between 7.30 and 8 am, come summer or winter. This early hour has a status symbol. Its origin lies in the DTC insisting that the schools must release its buses well before nine in the morning and three in the afternoon so that they are ready to ferry office traffic!

A second session is infra dig for a private unaided school, although in the cooler months, children can study better during the afternoons. Many government schools teach in two sessions, morning for the girls and afternoon for the boys. But the same Directorate of Education would not permit an unaided school to do this.

It gives no thought to the fact that the school buildings are used for only 1,260 hours, for 210 days, out of the total 8,760 hours in the year. How much more can one underutilise or waste an asset built with the help of charity?

Incidentally, there was nothing sacrosanct about Sunday until the advent of the British rule. For Muslims, Fridays are all important for prayers. Hindus prefer Thursdays. Bengalis do not like doing business on Thursdays; and until the 1950s, most shops in Kolkata remained closed until Friday afternoons. This is not to suggest any change except an appeal to utilise time and national assets better and to create more employment.

Some years ago a battle royal took place in Paris. The French trade unions were well-known for their rigidity and came in the way of clothiers working on Sundays, although it was alright for restaurants, florists and pharmacies to remain open. Louis Vuitton, the upmarket fashion goods company, bypassed the labour laws for the workers right to leisure by starting an exhibition on the top floor of its flagship store on Avenue des Champs Elysees.

Incidentally, the Industrial Disputes Act, which influences so much of the workers thinking in India, was given to us in April 1947, exactly four months before the British left India. Even the day for work and night for rest is a mindset. For example, in Norway, the day lasts for six months and night for the remaining six, which is why it is called the land of the midnight sun. The country is electrically lit on winter afternoons. Yet, the general sleep time is after 10 pm!

DYNAMICS OF MULTIPLYING EMPLOYMENT

PRODUCTIVE EMPLOYMENT for everyone fit to work should be the supreme goal of any economic strategy in India. Inducing green and white revolutions, promoting industries and building dams are all laudable activities but they should be treated as means towards achieving the end of productively employing every able-bodied Indian citizen.

The word 'productive' needs an explanation as well as emphasis. For our purpose it means comfortable survival in a competitive environment at market prices. A competitive environment is one wherein everyone is free to participate and no job is secure unless the value of the employee's work exceeds his or her cost. Many an employee protected by the Nehruvian ethics may not measure up to this criterion of competition. 'When in doubt, employ', was the 'mantra' of the past decades. However unnecessary the job, the fact of having found some employment appeared to many as an act of service in a poor nation. It was realised by a few that redundant employment was a burden on society. In government, the expense diverted funds from a productive investment and increased expenditure much of which was met by printing money which, in turn, caused inflation. In the private sector, the expense proved a drag on the employer's growth and progress. The collapse of communism in Europe exploded the myth about 'any employment anyhow'.

"At market prices" needs little elucidation. No subsidies, no levy price or quota and no restrictions on sale to anyone including for export. For example, there is no question of oilseeds being confined within the state of their harvest. Or, for that matter, no question of not shipping them if there was demand overseas.

The issue of the end and the means also needs clarification. The economic management has seldom been looked upon in a national perspective or harnessed for the sake of every Indian. The policymakers have been prisoners of class dogmas. Prof Mahalanobis, the Bengali scientist and statistician, was a socialist wedded to a planned economy exemplified by the Soviet experiment; whereas Dr Manmohan Singh, influenced by American capitalism stood for a free market economy. Over the decades, capitalists, whether private or government, have promoted mechanised factories, while socialists have protected unionised employment. Neither has worried about what happens to those who are not the beneficiaries of either a factory or a union. And an overwhelming number of Indians are not.

Due to the lack of a national focus, the dynamics of multiplying employment have been overlooked. There are many obstacles in the path of generating employment, whether they are hurdles in the transfer of goods from one state to another. An example was the lifting of the restrictions on the movement of molasses by the centre; since then the states have raised new objections. The lifting of restrictions on the movement of oilseeds out of Gujarat was a step in the right direction from this viewpoint.

To return to urban employment, the labour legislations in India are depressing. The way it is administered is destructive. It is seen at its worst in the states where the communists wield influence. The unionised employees no doubt get protection; in fact, such pampering that they need not really work and yet collect all benefits, including bonus at the maximum rate of 20 percent. The employer has no alternative but to lump it. There is no way he can separate a unionised employee unless the union for some unusual reason happens to help. No one with a tradition of entrepreneurship touches a new labour-intensive enterprise. In the process many a glorious opportunity to employ many is lost. Cheap labour is repeatedly mentioned as an Indian advantage. The pity is how little this opportunity is exploited. Instead, most new businesses are computerised and new factories are machine-intensive. Like industrial relations, the income tax laws also favour the machine. It attracts a generous depreciation allowance and can be virtually written off in a few years. In contrast, there is no tax incentive for employing people whose cost incidentally goes up every year. Nor can people be dispensed with as the machine can be sold off.

The state-owned development banks like the IDBI or the ICICI also favour the machine and neglect the man. They give attractive loans for building factories and acquiring plants but have no cells to finance labour-intensive manufacture. This is not to argue against mechanised manufacture or a plea to return to the 18th century. It is only an appeal for not missing entrepreneurial opportunities that do not happen to be preponderantly mechanical.

Hundreds of crores were spent on building "the temples of modern India" mostly in the public sector but also some by private investment. The missing link was the lack of a focus on employment as a supreme Indian priority. When the giant factories were first set up they took say Rs 50,000 capital outlay to create one job. Soon the figure rose to one lakh rupees. Today, it takes an investment of some ten lakh rupees to provide one productive job. This was a luxury in a poor country short of capital. In a society starved of employment, was it not a crime?

A comparable investment in agriculture, productively deployed, would spark a miracle. The pros and cons of industry versus agriculture are well known. It is, however, necessary to stress that manufacture is inherently a mechanical activity whereas farming is essentially an interplay between man and nature. And, therefore, up to a point, the more the men the better they can exploit nature. Another fundament to remember is that farming is useful for almost all talukas or blocks of the country, whereas industry has to be choosy about location if it is to succeed. In sponsoring agriculture, there is greater social justice among persons, between the two sexes, among talukas and between one state and another. Remember, all need employment but not everyone can uproot themselves and move to a factory site. Moreover, women are rarely welcome in large factories. Widespread agricultural growth is, therefore, a pre-condition of multiplying employment.

Plenty of information and a decision to set-up vocational training schools and polytechnics on a large scale are likely to expose the hollowness of a great portion of education in India. The enormous numbers of colleges that flourish and work up to three shifts produce graduates by the lakhs, but not many among these graduates are readily employable. The quality of education they have is no longer needed. The era of clerks and officers has passed. The computers are replacing them. Now only specifically-trained persons, whether as machine operators, artisans like carpenters or salesmen, chartered or business executives and accountants are required. An average graduate is unable to be of any use unless he begins his training all over again. And not everyone is good enough to be an executive or an accountant. The result of this entire mismatch is a gathering crowd of educated unemployed.

The tale of miseducation does not end here. The country's language policy is confused. Most political parties and most state governments are against the serious study of English from the primary stage. No doubt there are two sides to the coin. As a medium of expression one's mother tongue is ideal. As a foundation of pride, the national language is essential. Language as a means of communication and language as an aid to employment are two facets. Ironical as it is, an Indian language does not help many of its speakers and writers to get lucrative jobs. Be it the public or the private sector, the language of the bigger trade and industry is English. For example, most stenographers in Gujarat are from either Kerala or Tamil Nadu. It is very difficult to get a local stenographer who is proficient in English. And stenographers in Gujarati are unwanted by commerce.

The dynamics of employing the educated must, therefore, begin with a decision on India's language policy. There are families in India who spend a great deal on private tutors to make their sons proficient in English; for no other reason than the conviction that if the boys do not know English well, they would not get lucrative jobs.

MADARSAS CAN'T BE SECULAR

MODERNISING THE madarsa is a contradiction in terms. Madarsa is essentially a Muslim school, college, or university that is often part of a mosque. Chapter 3 of *The Oxford History of Islam*, written by Prof Mohammad Hashim Kamali, has defined the madarsa as a theological college. If such a college were ideal, it would not only teach the Holy Quran and the Hadith but also *fiqh* (Islamic jurisprudence), as interpreted by the four different schools of Sunni Islam, namely, Hanafi, Maliki, Shafii and Hanbali, to be located in four different corners of the same building. An outstanding example of such a madarsa is Al Azhar in Cairo built in the 14th century by Mamluk Sultan Hasan.

In the early centuries *ijtihad* or independent reasoning in Islamic theology was permitted. During the Abbasid Caliphate based in Baghdad, it was however felt that independent reasoning would lead to a contradiction of the universal acceptance that Islam was the final message delivered by the last prophet.

In contrast, Christianity always permitted independent reasoning. This liberty led to the Reformation Movement in the 16th century, spearheaded by Martin Luther of Germany and John Calvin of Switzerland. Islam had the vision to pre-empt its own scattering into many denominations. It prohibited *ijtihad* well in time. The Abbasids were Caliphs between 750 and 945 AD.

The Central Madarsa Board Bill, whose draft has reportedly been prepared for the HRD Ministry, would appear to be misplaced in this context. To expect to create a Central Madarsa Board along the lines of the CBSE is unrealistic and to fund the modernisation of the system would be a waste of the tax payers' money. For such religious seminaries to offer any education which could lead to the questioning of the tenets of Islam would not be possible.

Secular education is bound to lead to questioning or introducing parallel explanations. An example of this syndrome was Charles Darwin's 'Theory of Evolution' which cut at the root of the Biblical assumption that god created the world in six days and rested on the seventh. Surely, no *momin* would like such a thing to happen to Islam.

The avoidance of secular education is consistent with what Prophet Mohammad desired. The Prophet said that *ilm* or knowledge was of three kinds—the verses of the Quran, the Hadith and the lawful interpretation of both these. Any knowledge beyond these three was unnecessary.

A madarsa is located near a masjid since prayer and religious education are intertwined. This is in contrast to a convent or a missionary school. No matter how evangelical the mission, its school attracts students from all faiths. Such schools are affiliated with secular boards like CBSE, ICSE or the State

Boards, whereas the Central Madarsa Bill envisages a separate board.

Oxford and Cambridge began as Christian seminaries for prayer as well as religious education, including copying the Bible. A number of leading American universities were founded by Protestant missionaries. Muslims have also produced some extraordinary centres of learning in Baghdad and Cairo, but none of them was able to measure up to the challenges of the age of reason.

Muslim rulers dominated the Indian scene for centuries in the pre-modern era. Yet, no university worth the name came into being. The Aligarh Muslim University, the Osmania University (Hyderabad) and the Jamia Millia Islamia (Delhi) were established after the British rule began. Evidently, the community has been averse to education beyond the pale of theological studies. One must recall how on the morrow of Lord Macaulay's minutes on education, the *ulema* advised the Muslim youth to avoid Western science and English education. After the mutiny of 1857, this appeal became louder.

Until 1780, Muslims had monopolised all the important positions of state, as reported by Sir William Hunter in his book *The Indian Musalman.* He published a table showing the distribution of senior officers in the Bengal of a century later. Of all the gazetted jobs, 1338 were held by Europeans, 681 by Hindus, and Muslims had only 92 positions. Of these, 67 were either deputy collectors or *munsifs*. There was hardly any engineer or accountant.

Some years ago, Syed Shahabuddin, a Muslim politician, wrote in a letter to *The Pioneer* that if there was conflict between identity and development, the Muslims would choose the former. Earlier, Maulana Abul Kalam Azad held similar views.

Consistent with this indifference towards development, there was little need for modern education. Little wonder the ulema exhorted Muslims to avoid English education for fear that they would dilute, if not also compromise, the purity of their faith.

AUROBINDO'S LIFE DIVINE

ON 24 November 1926 at Pondicherry, Sri Aurobindo had his major vision of the divine which he called *siddhi*. Commenting on his greatness, the *Times Literary Supplement* wrote that he might prove to be one of the truly creative philosophers who gave a new thought and a new vision to mankind. The class of philosophers the journal had in mind included Plato, Kant, Hegel and Bergson. The same publication had elsewhere quoted Sir Francis Younghusband as having said that Sri Aurobindo's mystical magnum opus called *The Life Divine* was the greatest book which had been produced in his time (Page 143, *Sri Aurobindo* by Peter Heehs, OUP 2005).

It is not widely realised that yoga means not only a union of body and mind but ultimately also of the human with the divine. True, the latter union is extremely rare. Over the last several centuries, only two individuals are reputed to have been able to view the divine, namely, Sri Ramakrishna Paramhans and Sri Aurobindo. It is believed that both attained *mukti* or salvation; the former through *bhakti* and the latter with the help of *jnana* yoga. Their mystic experiences were at once similar and yet very different.

Sri Aurobindo was almost entirely educated in England over a period of fourteen years. In his second year at King's College, Cambridge, he completed his classical Tripos. Praising his essay on a comparison between Shakespeare and Milton written for the Tripos, Oscar Browning called it wonderful. The famous poet went on to say that in his thirteen years as an examiner, he had not come across such excellent papers as this student's. Sri Aurobindo passed the ICS examination but ducked out of the appointment by missing the horse riding tests. Nevertheless, his learning was versatile ranging from the Greek classics to Latin not to speak of Sanskrit and English poetry.

Politics and India's freedom had begun to stir Sri Aurobindo while in England. One of his biographers AB Purani has written that when he put his foot on the soil of India at Apollo Bundar, he experienced a tremendous peace. He proceeded straight to Baroda to take up the appointment which he had accepted from Maharajah Sayajirao before leaving England. He served the state for over 13 years until he was 35. During those years, Sri Aurobindo took keen interest in politics of Bengal especially through his brother Barin. Being in the Maharajah's service, he had to remain in the background until the British government decided to prosecute him for writing in *Bande Matram*, a journal founded by Bipin Chandra Pal.

In 1904, Sri Aurobindo started practising yoga five to six hours daily. He called this practice *sadhana*. Although he did take a few advanced lessons from one Yogi Vishnu Bhaskar Lele in 1907, the rest of his efforts all his life were his own. Incidentally, Sri Aurobindo attended the historic Surat

Congress of 1907. Incredibly, he was already looked upon as a leading light of the extremists. Bal Gangadhar Tilak was his only senior. Although he had taken to political activity like a fish to water, it disturbed his *sadhana*. On many a day he could not even practise yoga; he found this disturbing.

In May 1908, Sri Aurobindo, along with some others was arrested in the Alipore Bomb Case. He left his defence to Chittaranjan Das and busied himself with *sadhana* even if in full view of the prison inmates. Once when the Governor visited the jail, he remarked that Sri Aurobindo's eyes were like those of a mad man. Charu Chandra Dutt corrected him by saying that they were those of a karma yogi! There were times when Sri Aurobindo experienced *siddhi*, the attainment of seeing light much greater than experienced in our world. On occasions he heard the voice of Swami Vivekananda. During the trial in court, he saw Vasudeva and Narayan instead of the Magistrate and the Prosecutor. One day in the course of a stance, he was reported to have experienced the divine. Sri Aurobindo has written about how he was urgently removed to his solitary cell. In his own words, what happened then and day after day he was not impelled to say except that "He showed me His wonders" (AB Purani). Thereafter, he often asked the divine for an *aadesh* or instruction.

After being acquitted in the Alipore Bomb Case, Sri Aurobindo began editing journals called *Karamyogi* and *Dharma*. At the office one afternoon came an *aadesh*, "Go to Chandernagore". He obeyed immediately and reached the French colony the same evening. In less than two months, came yet another divine instruction which asked him to proceed to Pondicherry which he did on 31 March 1910 by a French boat named Dupleix. Despite a shortage of money, Sri Aurobindo was able to concentrate on his *sadhana* as well as writing, including his epic poem *Savitri*.

His devotee, later the legendary Mother named Mira, wife of Paul Richard, first called on Sri Aurobindo on 29 March 1914 along with her husband who was a French journalist. She had repeatedly dreamt of Lord Krishna. When she met Sri Aurobindo, she knew she had found the *avatar*. She had had mystical experiences since childhood. Soon, World War I drew her back to Europe. She could not return to Pondicherry until April 1920; this time never to leave until her end in 1973. Her life was dedicated to the spread of the message of Sri Aurobindo. Developing into a versatile organiser, she created the entire complex of institutions and the ashram.

Sri Aurobindo mingled more and more with the divine and found the ultimate success or *siddhi* on 24 November 1926. In his own words, life is all yoga. Moreover, his sadhana was not merely for his own self-realisation but also for the gain of mankind (Heehs page 96). After the *siddhi* he confined himself to his apartment in the ashram and met no more than seven or eight outsiders in the course of the following 24 years. He was no organiser. It was the Mother who, in the celebration of Sri Aurobindo, played the role reminiscent of Saints Peter and Paul for Jesus Christ or Ashoka in the spread of Buddhism.

MILITARY: DEFENCE IN DEPTH

VICTORIES IN the cricket series have done a great deal for India's national morale. On most other fronts, we were on the defensive. Pakistanis attacked Mumbai and New Delhi and we were able to do little. On the economic front, there was a meltdown.

If there was a single outstanding reason behind the victories, it was the captaincy of Mahendra Singh Dhoni, the like of whom India had not seen for a long time.

With growing competition, it is logical that coaches should begin insisting on their trainees to bowl as well as bat. So far the approach has been to concentrate and consolidate the department of the game for which a youngster shows aptitude. Many years ago, there was little by way of systematic training from a young age; only a touch-up for adult players. Just as until 20 years ago, fielding in Indian cricket was taken for granted as incidental to playing and not as a vital factor for being included in a team.

The next stage of evolution is for a bowler to be able to bowl with both arms. Since the beginning of the game, there have been ambidextrous cricketers. Some of them like Vinoo Mankad bowled with the left arm but batted with the right. Others did the opposite, like Sourav Ganguly who batted with the left and bowled with his right. Quite a few fielders can throw the ball to the wicket-keeper with either arm.

Different batsmen are vulnerable to different bowling; the greater therefore the variety in the attacking armour, the brighter the chances of victory. Quite often it also depends on the condition of the pitch. If everyone is coached and practised to be an ambidextrous bowler, there would be many more bowlers at the captain's disposal.

With the same logic, each batsman should be trained from childhood to bat with both hands so that different situations can be countered with left or right-handed defence. For example, an inswing or a leg break by a right arm bowler can be better defended by a left-handed batsman. If the suggested ambidextrousness could be introduced, a team of eleven heads would field 21 batsmen, 20 bowlers, 10 super fielders and a wicket-keeper, adding up to 52 versatile players.

The tooth to tail ratio concept was first observed in World War I. The British army had ten support men for every fighting soldier. The support included medicos, engineers, drivers and signallers. Since these men were not meant to fire, they were called the tail while the soldier with a rifle or a machine gun was treated as a tooth. The German army's ratio during the same war was that for every tooth, there were only four in the tail which means the Germans were two and a half times more efficient than the British. An average non-bowler fielder amounts to tail, not tooth, when his side is fielding. Similarly, a pure bowler is a part of the tail when his team is batting. In fact, he is called the tail even in cricket! It needs hardly be clarified that a tooth is for biting while a tail is at most useful in chasing flies.

An old mindset about the batting order still lingers. That better the batsman, the earlier in the order he should be sent. The result is that the weaker batsmen have to bat often under pressure of time or score; they do not have the range of strokes required to score and without reckless risk. It is, therefore, expedient to send the weaker ones early provided the innings has started well and there is no pressure. By the same token, in the event there are runs to score quickly or wickets to save the team from defeat, the quality batsmen should be more useful. In the army, this would be called defence in depth!

The approach to bowling also needs a change. As distinct from a Test match, an ODI does not require the bowler to be aggressive and go for getting the batsmen out. Instead, the broad bowling strategy should be to bowl with immaculate accuracy and good length on the middle stump reminiscent of Bapu Nadkarni who bowled maiden over after maiden over, often without taking any wicket. In an ODI, it is the batsmen who have to be in a hurry to score runs. Even if the bowler reduces his speed in order to achieve accuracy, there would be nothing lost. It is the batsmen who must hit out and hopefully get out.

So much so, that in an ODI, it is the bowling side which must be called the defence and the batsmen the attack. Quite the opposite of Test matches wherein traditionally the bowlers are called the attack, whether spin or speed; and batsmen the defenders.

One great anomaly is that India with its 105 crore people

is represented by an eleven-men team; whereas Australia, Sri Lanka, West Indies et al, with much smaller populations, also have similar teams. Should not the five zones of India be allowed to play Tests and international ODI's so that more Indian youth get an opportunity?

GOVERNANCE ALONE MATTERS

MANY YEARS ago, the Home Ministry informed Parliament that it had received recommendations from the public for the creation of several new states. Although no state government had made a suggestion, the proposals ranged from Bhojpur, Coorg, Gorkhaland, and Koshalanchal to Mithilanchal. Many of these recommendations were frivolous but they did reflect discontent over the declining quality of governance. When the Bihar fodder scam was in the news, it was not crucial whether the chief minister had pocketed Rs 600 crore; what was important was that he had failed to govern. Not to say that his predecessors were much better administrators. The government at Patna had generally been poor and unstable since the general elections of 1967.

In this regard, UP was a bigger bird of the same feather. The residents of the two states had been steadily migrating to other states for employment even if it be at below subsistence wage; which, in turn, sharply undercut the local workmen.

This was sad when one noted that most of the paragraphs of Chapter VII of the States Reorganization Commission Report (SRC) 1955, spoke about the Five-Year Plan and the effect of the size of the state on development.

Since Independence, we were all concerned about poverty in India regardless of how much we were able to reduce it. But since the slogan of 'India Shining' was launched, even that concern had been pushed to the backburner. Meanwhile, other than the urban middle and upper classes, most people were marking time or getting poorer. In any case, the contrast between the common man's plight and the upwardly-mobile Indian has become painfully sharp. The TV is helping to exaggerate the differences. Raj Thackeray was not the only rabble-rouser who cashed in on the resulting discontent. The Maoists were much greater beneficiaries of the 'Groaning India'.

The contrast between the rich and the poor is not confined to urban and rural or between the professionals and the uneducated. It is equally sharp between region and region, state and state. If there be five regions of the country, the east and the central are languishing. The north, comprising Punjab, Haryana and Delhi, the west and the south are flourishing. The people from Bihar and UP who go to Mumbai, Delhi or cities in Gujarat, do so because they are desperate for employment. Many of them work for a pittance. The desperation is such that Brahmins from Bihar are seen tending and cleaning Sulabh Shauchalayas in cities like Vadodara.

As time passes, the freedom struggle and all that patriotic fervour it aroused are receding into distant memory. Globalization and free trade are taking a toll of nationalism; so is the increasing consumerism and the lure of earning money. The youth of tomorrow may well become self-centered enough to ignore the importance of national integrity. A time may come, several decades hence, when the youth of a prosperous state will question the need to pay for carrying the burden of backward states as part of their country. It is noteworthy that both Bihar and UP get central subsidies through the Finance Commission for not being able to raise taxes sufficient to meet their essential revenue expenditure. A Tamil youth can question the need for his state to pay for the inefficiency of the government at say, Lucknow or Patna.

The questioning youth, in his misguided intolerance, may cite the example of the Soviet Union which spontaneously decided to allow its 14 republics or provinces to go their separate way. Yugoslavia was yet another unfortunate case of provinces seceding one by one, beginning with Slovenia followed by Croatia, Bosnia Herzegovina, Macedonia and now part-province Kosovo. Nationalism can no longer be taken for granted as a safeguard of a country's unity. Until the 18th century, religion was the ideology which supported the monarchs of Europe. Thereafter, nationalism became the binding factor of European countries.

In contrast, communism considered the nation-state an instrument of exploitation of the poor in the hands of the rich. It exhorted the workers of the world to unite. Internationalism became its slogan. India has plenty of communists. It also has many *ulema* whose commitment is to the world *ummah* in preference to any loyalty to the country. The nation-state has no place in Islamic ideology; nor do national frontiers matter much to them. The confusion is worse confounded by the fact of Pakistan and Bangladesh being neighbours. The safeguards of national integrity, therefore, are fewer in India than say in the USA, Japan or even the formerly communist China which has 93 percent people of the Han race.

Indians have to be more careful in their endeavour to remain a united country. They should not, as some of its elitists do, dream of the European Union which has now one currency, one visa and so on. Loose talk about a confederation of South-Asian countries would only dilute the focus on Indian unity. In the ultimate analysis, advice like this would have limited value. The main responsibility would lie on how our states provide a structural balance to the Indian federation. No state should be too large or dominant due to its big population. On the other hand, no state should be so small as to be economically unviable. The central dole to states should be minimised. Certainly UP and Bihar should help to create surpluses rather than deficits. Uneven growth and prosperity must cause inter-state envy and tension. In other words, if another SRC is appointed, its primary duty would be to redesign such a federal map that the states would lend themselves to efficient governance. As the future unfolds, language, caste and even religion are likely to decline in importance. Economic efficiency would be the key to the national integrity of India.

THE 'GREAT CALCUTTA KILLING'

NOT MANY Indians remember or know that on 16 August 1946 began the bloodiest and the biggest state-sponsored riot in the country's history. The riots took place between August 16 and 20 in Calcutta, the capital of undivided Bengal, whose premier was Huseyn Shaheed Suhrawardy, the Muslim League leader in the assembly. Incidentally, he later became prime minister of Pakistan.

August 16 was planned by the League led by Jinnah to launch a 'Direct Action Day' to convince the British that Hindus and Muslims could not coexist in the same country and, hence, India must be partitioned. The tactical manifesto was distributed to the League activists; it had 23 points as reproduced by Justice GD Khosla in his famous work *Stern Reckoning* (OUP India, 1949). A few of the points read as follows: "Destroy Hindus and drive all Hindus out of India. All transport should be used for battle against Hindus. Hindu women and girls should be raped, kidnapped and converted into Muslims from October 18, 1946. Hindu culture should be destroyed". The Calcutta District Muslim League published on 13 August 1946 an elucidation of the programme quoted above. It clarified that the Direct Action Day was to be conducted in the name of the Quran, the holy month of Ramzan, the Battle of Badr and the Holy Prophet.

On 22 August, Bengal Governor Sir Frederick Burrows wrote a detailed report to Viceroy Lord Wavell on what came to be known as the Great Calcutta Killings. To quote Burrows for August 16: "The trouble had already assumed the communal character which it was to retain throughout. At the time it was mainly in the northern half of the city. Later reports indicate that the Muslims were in an aggressive mood from early in the day and that their processions were well-armed with lathis, iron rods and missiles".

On August 17 Burrows wrote: "This tour convinced me that the reports that I had received of the seriousness of the situation had erred on the side of underestimation. I observed very great damage to property and streets littered with corpses. I can honestly say that parts of the city on Saturday morning were as bad as anything I saw when I was with the Guards on the Somme (the bloodiest battle of WWI fought in Belgium wherein the total casualties were estimated to be 12,65,000 soldiers). The feeling was entirely communal".

The highlight of August 18 in the Governor's letter was: "I made another tour of inspection, this time with the Army Commander and the Chief Minister, covering large areas in the south and south-east of the city which I had not visited before. The chief minister showed an exasperating preoccupation with the sufferings undergone by members of his own community". The slaughter over the first few days was so widespread that

Burrows could not give any authoritative casualty figures. Guided mainly by hospital figures, he guessed 2,000 dead at the very least. But in the mayhem, most of the dead got nowhere near a hospital. In fact, no one was available to clear the dead bodies until "the Army came to my rescue on the basis of Rs 5 a body to volunteers", the Governor wrote.

The Statesman, then a British-owned daily, on August 22, wrote: "The group of incompetents, or worse, who owing to their office necessarily bear primary responsibility for the criminal carnage in Calcutta, a catastrophe of scope unprecedented in India's history, have been insufficiently seen or heard in these grim days. We mean the Ministry". BK Nehru, in his memoirs *Nice Guys Finish Second* (Viking, 1997) commented: "This massacre of the Hindus and Sikhs by Muslims was well-organized and directed personally by HS Suhrawardy".

Headlined "Calcutta's Ordeal", *The Statesman* on August 20 had written: "The origin of the appalling carnage and loss in the capital of a great Province, we believe the worst communal rioting in India's history, was a political demonstration by the Muslim League". *The Modern Review*, an eminent monthly of the time wrote in its September 1946 issue: "Soon the city was ablaze from North to South and from East to West. The Hindus of Calcutta gradually realised that denial of police aid was part of the programme. It was not as if there was not enough force at the disposal of the authorities. Armed police and Anglo-Indian armed sergeants were there in plenty, sitting idle and twiddling their thumbs. The situation soon became precarious for the Hindus all over Calcutta".

What MA Jinnah said, as quoted by Justice Khosla, was the most authoritative declaration on the killing: "What we have done today is the most historic act in our history. Never have we in the whole history of the League done anything except by constitutional methods and by constitutionalism. But now we are obliged and forced into this position. This day we bid goodbye to constitutional methods". So Machiavellian, though Jinnah at least began life as a barrister and he had remained a constitutionalist for the greater part of his career.

A much worse example is the email sent out by the Indian Mujahideen: "Hindus have no compassion in their religion. It is the duty of Muslims to wage a jihad against Hindu oppressors and it is the Hindu who is a terrorist". In this day and age, the email invokes Ghori and Ghaznavi to settle the score with Hindus. Imagine if people like this came anywhere near power, even in a state government, what would happen? They may make the Great Calcutta Killings appear merely a fracas.

50 YEARS: PAST AND FUTURE

NATIONALISM IS essential for welding a society into one and then galvanising its energies in the single direction of progress. Unless all or most citizens feel possessed by a nationalist priority, it is difficult for a nation to achieve a synergy or a collective energy which, so to say, results in 2+2 equalling 5 and not merely 4. It is this additional generation of 5 instead of 4 which takes the country forward instead of marking time.

On balance, India has marked time over the past fifty years. If the economy has got industrialised, its burgeoning population has diluted, if not nullified, the achievement. The average Indian still remains poor. One out of two Indians is illiterate. Many more than half our womenfolk are not literate. Most countries of Asia have gone ahead of India, be it China, Korea, Indonesia or Malaysia.

Without the unity and the synergy that nationalism gives, these countries would not have taken their strides forward. The bond and the vibrancy that the spirit gives are essential for a country to become modern. Germany and Japan are the best instances of what national determination can help to achieve. The Soviet Union and its communism, or non-nationalism, offers the opposite example.

It is true that China is dominantly a one-language, one-race country. Nevertheless, it was distraught until the revolution which ended in 1949. Mao Zedong was first a Chinese, second a nationalist and then a communist. He did not sacrifice Chinese interests upon the altar of communism. For instance, among his first steps as head of China was to assert its suzerainty over Tibet.

India did the opposite. It conceded China's claim presumably for the sake of international peace and goodwill. In the bargain, it lost a valuable buffer state as well as discounted its image among the other neighbouring countries. Instead of welding itself into a vibrant nation-state on the basis of its all-pervading (except perhaps in the Garo, Khasi, Mizo and Naga regions) Hindu ethos, India was distracted by internationalism as well as trans-nationalism.

The former led to the placation of those whose gods resided in either Moscow or Peking (now Beijing); whose religion said that the nation-state was an instrument of exploitation and that the state would wither away. The latter led to the pampering of those whose souls lived in either Mecca or Islamabad although their bodies resided in India. Socialism and secularism have been the two banes of Indian progress.

How could the population be controlled when the devotees of these had to be against family planning? Poverty is fertile soil for socialism and large families are a key to perpetuating penury. Similarly, the Indian version of secularism flourished on pampering those who believed in polygamy which is the antithesis of family planning. Large families mean not only poor members but generally uneducated people too.

Such policies served partisan interests. The Congress party flourished but neither the country nor its citizens. Socialism made the rich richer and the poor became poorer. Secularism did not improve the lot of the Muslims who remained as uneducated, unemployed and backward as before. National interests were sacrificed for party gains in several other spheres, one instance being the size of states.

The size of Uttar Pradesh was retained by the 1956 Commission in order to ensure a large enough base for Jawaharlal Nehru in his endeavour to remain prime minister. The late socialist leader Ashok Mehta had told this to my father in 1957.

As a consolation to the Morarji Desai lobby, the ludicrous jumbo-state of Bombay was formed; it rolled into all the Marathi as well as Gujarati-speaking districts of India. It is worth recalling that Justice Syed Fazl Ali and Pandit Hriday Nath Kunzru were personal friends of Jawaharlal Nehru. The third member of the Commission, Sardar KM Panikkar, had differed and recommendid that Uttar Pradesh was too large.

To win most of the seats in UP was, however, also important. Sixteen odd percent of the voters were Muslim; appeasing the community leaders was, therefore, necessary. This is the source of minority pampering after Independence. To begin with, Jawaharlal Nehru's focus was fairly nationalist. His 1948 speech to the students of the Aligarh Muslim University was a specimen. He told them that the entire long history of India was their heritage and they must identify themselves with the new free India. What else was the essence of cultural nationalism or Hindutva? But the Congress policy changed as the 1952 general elections approached. The Muslim leaders had to be pampered. What was expedient in UP had to be followed all over India. So, pampering became a national policy for the Congress Party.

Looking ahead is more meaningful than looking back. History is no doubt useful for getting the direction of a futurological projection. Yet history has been defined as the selection and interpretation of facts about the past that are relevant for the future. What is not relevant for the future but is yet interesting is story and not history! Most of us are broadly aware of what happened during the first fifty years after independence and why. The Nehruvian ethos was weak. Jawaharlal Nehru had vision but lacked strength. He, therefore, opted out of competing with the world. In the name of non-alignment, he snugly stayed by the side of the Soviet superpower. In return for the snug protection, India led the so-called non-aligned nations in the UN General Assembly in lobbying against the USA.

In the economic sphere also India opted out of competition. It resorted to import substitution on the one hand and barter trade on the other. Rupee agreements were not confined to the Soviet Union but also signed with Egypt, Iraq, Syria, Yugoslavia, East Germany, Hungary, Poland and others. Whether the Indian economy lost or gained by this type of trade is a matter of controversy. What is not debatable is that it reduced the country's competitiveness.

The industrialists who were nurtured in this Nehruvian incubator were like Ranji Trophy cricketers rather than Test players, club footballers rather than Olympians. Not entirely their fault but nevertheless true. Another factor that retarded them as well as the entire community of traders was the so-called progressive income tax and its vexatious rates. This socialistic phenomenon prevented the accumulation of white or official wealth. A large portion of the economic surplus of the private sector got dyed in black.

The result is that today neither the industrialists nor their corporations have investible funds required to promote industrial projects on an international scale. Even where they have collaborations, instead of flourishing, they are tending to sell out to the foreigner. Peugot and DCM-Daewoo are just two instances. Their weakest link generally is not money but management. There are excellent individual managers but few managerial teams without which mega industries cannot be built or run.

The ethos is dominantly proprietary rather than corporate. The dominant shareholder, whether holding a majority or a minority of the shares, generally looks upon himself as the owner in the spirit of a feudal lord. The managers are supposed to obey him implicitly. Another handicap is that, for the size of India, there are not enough entrepreneurs. The reason probably is that the commanding heights of the economy were to be held by the State or the public sector under the Nehruvian prescription.

On the credit side, India has a whole *bania* class, whether by caste or by inclination. The number of potential entrepreneurs, therefore, is infinite. They are born businessmen and even the average among them is strong on arithmetic and finance. He can read money like the back of his hand. This is a great Indian strength although so far it has not been sufficiently exposed to world business.

In fact, so far it might have acted as a handicap. The reason is that if an entrepreneur is too conscious of the rate of return on his money, he is unlikely to risk it on a long gestation project. Can one think of an Indian entrepreneur doing what Pepsi Cola has done? Invest huge sums and also lose them by the billion in order to establish the product in the Indian market. In contrast, what Parle must have realised from the sale of Thums Up was that it could earn a much better return in the foreseeable future after this sale.

It appears that India has lost the industrial race. It was late to start on its industrial revolution and its efforts were half-hearted. This situation came about because of the British yoke which did not encourage any production that would compete with British goods. There is, however, nothing to lose heart over. Prior to the industrial revolution, essentially over the 19th century, the primary sector was the dominant economic sector. What grew on land, what could be mined from below the ground and what could be caught from the sea were what mattered. Thereafter, what began to matter most was the secondary or the industrial sector. The industrially advanced economies were the developed countries.

The coming 50 years or more may well belong to the tertiary or the services sector. The manufacturing sector would remain important but not dominant, rather like agriculture, mining and fishing which continue to be important but not dominant since the industrial revolution succeeded and manufacturing occupied the centre-stage. During the next five decades, in all likelihood, services led by computers and information technology (IT) are likely to take the centre-stage of economy.

By defeating world champion Gary Kasparov, the supercomputer Deep Blue demonstrated the dimensions of the Information Technology revolution we are passing through. Scientists believe that it would be as path-breaking as the industrial revolution which began two centuries ago. What enormous economic leaps Europe and America made and how quickly!

India, as we have seen, was late and slow. It is now no use chasing the tail of the developed world. The last chance to catch up was when Germany and Japan began soon after 1945. It does not mean that India should not set up industries; it should make every effort so long as the scale and size are world-class. Equally, efforts should be redoubled to promote agriculture, mining, fishing etc. But the national thrust should be to ride the Information Technology revolution and aspire to be a frontrunner.

India is already in the midst of computers and the international trade in software. Its young men and women are already acknowledged as first-rate programmers. Fifty thousand new jobs are being created every year quite spontaneously. Many believe that in five to seven years the country could become a software superpower. Some go to the extent of predicting that computers would do for India what oil did for West Asia.

Such is the opportunity for India to catch up on the lost opportunities and become as developed an economy as any over the next 25 years or so. That should become the national mission. The next fifty years could then be a golden age in Indian history.

KOLKATA: A CITY WITH A SOUL

LISTENING TO the debate at the Indian School, I was reminded of what I used to say in our early years in Delhi. Having lived in Calcutta (now Kolkata) for a total of thirty-eight years, we arrived in Delhi at the end of March 1982. In some ways we experienced a cultural shock. If we compare or contrast Calcutta with Delhi we can explore what is an urban soul. Calcutta is a metropolis with a soul. To illustrate this point, in Calcutta what matters is *what you are*. By contrast, in Delhi what matters is *what you have*. Are you a judge? Are you an IAS officer, an MP, a minister, or someone with a great deal of authority? For big wealth to be recognised, one has to be a very prominent industrialist like Birla or Ambani. Anyone smaller runs around a minister rather than a minister running around him. In short, what matters in Delhi is power. So long as one has it one is pampered. On retirement, quite often, even known subordinates do not have the inclination to recognise the person for he has ceased to be powerful.

In Calcutta, no matter how rich or powerful one is, it does not really matter. A secretary to the government or a minister could become a member of a club like the Bengal Club, the Calcutta Club, the Tollygunje Club or the Saturday Club, if he or she is socio-culturally acceptable, well-mannered and generally a nice person. Otherwise, the VIP would be requested to withdraw his application. If he does not withdraw he would be blackballed or rejected. In many ways Calcutta has the best of both worlds; the goodness of a village as well as the merits of a metropolis. One may not be in contact with a friend for years but if one phones him in the middle of the night, he would come to your help because he feels that he is not only your friend but also a fellow citizen. On the other hand, being a large and old city, most of the facilities of a metropolis are available. Such a wonderful combination of the rural and the urban is probably not to be experienced anywhere else.

One plausible explanation for Calcutta evolving such a soul may be the cultural dominance of the Bengalis in a special sense. With few exceptions, most people in Calcutta implicitly accept the Bengalis to be the most cultured. The Marwari may be much richer but when it comes to culture, he bows to the Bengali. Some people from north India may be exceptions to this rule but then they are disliked. Despite their wealth, Marwaris are not resented because they seldom challenge the cultural superiority of the Bengalis. By the same token, the middle and upper-level Bengali presumes that he is culturally superior to everyone except the European. I grew up in a Bengali locality of south Calcutta. I took the trouble to speak Bengali as far as possible. I found acceptance by Bengali families but I do not think that I would pass the test of cultural equality. In that sense, I would remain below the best.

All in all, if the soul of Calcutta is to be defined, it could be called Anglo-Bengali or Bengali flavoured by nostalgia of the British era. Incidentally, about half the population of the city is non-Bengali and until 1921 it was the capital of India. Moreover, Bihar and Orissa were parts of the Bengal Presidency and large numbers also came from eastern UP in search of livelihood. After the British left, most business went into Marwari hands. Also, there were a significant number of people from Kerala and Tamil Nadu as well as the Punjab and Gujarat. There are many Muslims but a large proportion of them are Urdu speaking. There are many Christians and Anglo-Indians but none of these communities has ever tried to supersede the Anglo-Bengali flavour of the city's spirit.

Coming to Delhi, perhaps there is a distinct difference between Shahjahanabad and old Delhi on the one hand and the new or south Delhi on the other. Raisina Hill, where the Rashtrapati Bhavan is situated, began to come into prominence in 1931. Delhi grew into essentially a capital city to which people came and went, be they bureaucrats or diplomats, or politicians. Such a milieu does not normally lend itself to evolving a soul. The commerce in south Delhi grew from the patronage of an expanding government, with wealth legitimate or illegitimate, especially after the Avadi session of the Congress in 1955, when the government adopted a socialistic pattern of society as policy. The public sector headquarters, the permits issued for setting up even private industries across the country were mostly centred in Delhi. The childhood and adolescence of Delhi, therefore, was crude and materialistic; hardly congenial for anything to do with a soul or spirit. It is possible that even today old Delhi does have a culture and a tradition. However, because of some 600 years of Sultan and Badshah rule, the character of the culture was led by Muslims. The Partition in 1947 interrupted this Muslim leadership because the elite mostly emigrated to Pakistan. Only the commoners remained; they had to struggle for their survival and had little leisure for nurturing the soul.

Nevertheless, we have seen Delhi changing since we arrived in 1982. Over the last twenty-five years the wealth accumulation is gradually helping to create a class who have interest in culture. The second generation or the children of those who make quick money have now some leisure to cultivate culture. Despite this very welcome evolution, there is still an undercurrent of insecurity probably related to the innumerable invasions that Delhi, as well as its surroundings, have suffered over the centuries. This insecurity calls for winding up of transactions quickly: who knows whether or not there will be a tomorrow? This apprehension does not lead to the growth of an ongoing goodwill which is an important facet of a mature soul.

AGHA IQBAL MIRZA, MY TEACHER

MY LESSON in conversational Urdu would be over in the evening by about 7:30. It was cool being early December (most probably 1977) and I offered my teacher Ahmed Khan a whisky soda for the first time. He was a modern person who wore trousers and shirts; an undergraduate who spoke English fluently. In the course of a chat over the drink, he happened to call Sheikh Abdullah an opportunist for having made up with New Delhi and become the chief minister again. I did not agree with Khan and went on to say that perhaps Sheikh Sahib had realised that Islam could not be the basis of a modern state; Pakistan had not held together and had broken up in 1971. Moreover, the Sheikh might have also reconciled himself to Kashmir being too small to be an independent republic; hence his release from prison and return to power.

Ahmed felt that the break-up of Pakistan had been engineered by New Delhi and had, therefore, no lesson to teach on Islam as a basis of a state. Fair enough, that was his view. Our debate was calm and easy through the second chhota peg. Thereafter, Ahmed seemed to get animated to tell me that Islam was 'no joke'. It was the most comprehensive code for human life. Sooner or later, it would spread to every nook and corner of the world. It was the most modern prescription as it gave property and inheritance rights to women 1,400 years ago. I listened with interest because he was talking with conviction. Although I did enquire as to why there was a widespread impression that in orthodox Muslim families, the women were not taught much beyond reading the Holy Quran and saying their prayers.

Ahmed got provoked and became more forceful. He asserted that the great faith had an extraordinarily integrated strategy. The cornerstone was fellow-feeling, brotherhood and unity. The purpose was to carry the message of Allah to all mankind. And it was the simple folk who were likely, in large numbers, to welcome the message. Education was, therefore, not of overriding importance. In fact, too much of it was likely to induce debate, dispute and dissidence. This, he said, is what happened to Christianity. Whereas, a simple dedicated mother is likely to ensure simple faithful children and rear more children cheerfully than an educated woman.

Numbers were a key to making the acceptance of the message universal. Hence, family planning was not permitted. Polygamy could only help numbers, Ahmed went on. Often it made the need felt for aphrodisiacs of which the Unani School of medicine had the best variety. Whether this was true or not, I am still not sure, but my animated teacher certainly aroused my interest in the Muslim frame of reference.

Until that fascinating evening, my interest in learning how to speak simple Urdu was merely to be able to pronounce

Hindustani words better. For my school final or matriculation in 1952, I had elementary Hindi as an additional subject. But that had not enabled me to speak the language either correctly or fluently. I had heard that the gateway to a good beginning was through Urdu. So, when my intention to eventually shift from Calcutta to Delhi began to crystalise, I began to look for a teacher probably around the middle of 1977. I had no contacts suitable for finding a modern educated Muslim who could teach me to speak Urdu. A *maulvi* would be traditional and unfamiliar with the kind of subjects I could chat about. Moreover, he might not have the English to translate for me.

One afternoon, the publisher of an Urdu journal in Patna, a Mr Zaman, dropped into my office. His object was to get to know me and then seek advertisements. I happened to request him to recommend a suitable Urdu teacher. The result was a call from Ahmed Khan a few days later. He claimed he was of Afghan origin although he was of a slight build no more than 5 feet 3 inches tall. He had pleasant manners, a quick wit and was an interesting conversationalist. He had a wife, two daughters and a son and, therefore, needed to do business. He hoped to get a contact or two through me which was more than the salary I proposed to pay him.

Soon began my education in conversational Urdu. Ahmed would come to the house and spend an hour or two just talking. I spoke most of the time and he corrected my mistakes; he also helped with new words and expressions. Sometime later he began talking of his uncle who was a senior doctor in a public hospital in Karachi. How much better off people were in Pakistan! That he was in acute need he had told me frequently. One evening, Ahmed looked delighted as he declared that he had obtained the visas and the family was migrating to Karachi for good. Before eventually leaving, he was gracious enough to introduce me to an acquaintance of his. Agha Iqbal Mirza would now take Ahmed's place as my Urdu *ustaad* (teacher).

Mirza made it clear soon enough that unlike Ahmed Khan he was a Mughal; his ancestors came to India not from Afghanistan but from Uzbekistan. Babur had set off from Samarkand in the same region. He was a BA from Delhi College, later known as the Maulana Azad College. His grandfather had been the *kotwal* (police chief) of Delhi, presumably of only the Shahjahanabad area. He had begun life as an agent of a private airline company of which there were many in the 1940s of Calcutta and eastern India. Mirza had not done well in business. Nevertheless, he was upright, honest and quite proud. He preferred to dress in a lounge suit with a bow tie. In Calcutta he lived with his two brothers and a sister; all the four siblings had never married! In the intellectual sphere, Agha Iqbal had translated a bunch of Urdu short stories into English. The work was published by the Writers Workshop of Professor Lal, a well-known Calcutta personality.

I could go on talking to Mirza for hours and we tried to meet at least twice a week when I was not travelling out of Calcutta. He tried to explain to me the origin of words. The verbs were all from *khadi boli* or Hindi as used in the western districts of UP, like Agra. The grammar was Hindi except for the plurals which often depended upon whether the noun was of Arabic or Persian origin. More than one *sanam* (beloved) was *asnaam*, plural of *khabar* (news) *akhbaar*. That was Arabic. Nouns of Persian ancestry like *khayaal* (thought) became *khayaalaat*. Urdu was indeed a grand piano with a wider range of sounds than any other language. It had two K's (or a K and a Q), two Kh's, two G's, two H's, two J's and four varieties of Z's.

Mirza was able to make me realise all this and more without my learning a single letter of the alphabet to read or write.

He often gave glimpses of esoteric expressions. For instance, *intezaar* was a common word; *muntezir* or the person waiting was less common but *muntezar* or the awaited person was very rarely used and most people were perhaps unaware of its existence.

Although he did not drink, he had quite a modern, unorthodox outlook. He did feel though that all Muslims should fast during the Ramzan month, though he himself did not as he had crossed the age of 60. He had no regrets about not having been to Pakistan. He said he had heard that in that country dogs were fed well but were not allowed to bark. In India, it was the opposite. One could say or speak what one liked but conditions were poorer. This probably reflected his preoccupation with his own debts and his penury. One of the few traits he shared with Ahmed Khan was an implicit presumption that the society owed him a living and the world was bound to keep him comfortable. If he was not well-off, the fault lay less with him and more with the people around him. I somewhat resented both my teachers for this attitude. When I thought I had hit upon the possible explanation for this presumptuousness many years later, my pique subsided.

The curiosity aroused then led to a continual search for the answer. Only recently did it occur to me that the Judaic ethos tends to assume that God made people equal. It is the imperfect environment on earth which makes them unequal. Society lacks equity. The leaders or the better-off richer people often bear an uneasy conscience about the poor and the miserable. Little wonder that the European and American visitors to India are shocked by the misery of the poorest Indians. They find it difficult to reconcile themselves to the sharp contrast between the rich and the poor. By the same token probably, the lesser-off among Christians or Muslims consider it their right to be helped by the society which makes them unfortunately unequal.

Khan and Mirza expected the world to help them in this. What emerged from these thoughts was that liberty and equality stand at opposite ends. The slogan of the French Revolution, liberty equality fraternity, has perhaps helped to conceal the contradiction or at least delay a debate. Liberty means freedom, for example, to earn, save and bequeath as much as one can. Equality, on the other hand, requires that the earnings are distributed either voluntarily or through social or state intervention, like progressive income tax whereby the more one earns, the higher the rate of the levy.

Christianity spontaneously tried to narrow the differences between the rich and the poor with the help of social services like free or near-free education and medicare. Think of all the schools, colleges and hospitals that are run by the missionaries like the Society of Jesus. Islam had its system of *zakat* whereby every Muslim was required to donate annually two and a half percent of his wealth. The money raised was redistributed to the Muslim poor.

The Hindu ethos is based on *karma* (actions) and *bhagya* (fate), cause and effect; as you sow so shall you reap. Each person has the liberty to enjoy the fruit of his/her fate which is the result of his/her deeds whether in this life or a previous incarnation. There is no obligation to redistribute; there is no spontaneous method of trying to equalise. There is no conscience about someone being poor or miserable for that is his *bhagya* based on his *karma*. Similarly, a poor person may seek help but cannot expect response as his right. He is basically reconciled that the cause of his problem lies in his own deeds. If the rich Hindu is charitable, it is out of sympathy, or perhaps as a way of getting social acclaim but not as a matter of conscience or duty. So much for liberty!

When I decided to move to Delhi, Mirza said he would also move. For quite a while I thought he was joking. In Calcutta he lived in a flat with his siblings on Congress Exhibition Road in Park Circus. Where would he reside in Delhi? I needed to pay him only Rs700 per month. This was early 1982 and I did not see how he could manage. Before long, I helped find him a quarter with a helpful MP friend in Feroze Shah Road and then got him a job in the Congress office as an Urdu/English translator. Ahmed Patel, the treasurer of the Party was very helpful. To begin with, Mirza and I were both freer in Delhi. We had long chats. He was not curious to know anything about me except perhaps now and then about my business. The questions were, therefore, almost all mine and they became more candid as our acquaintance grew. Once there was considerable controversy in the newspapers about fire crackers and sweets being distributed in the wake of a Pakistani victory in a cricket match against India. I asked Mirza point blank: why are so many Muslims in India pro-Pak? And if they are, why did they not migrate?

His reply to my words was a counter question. Do you think that the idols you bow before in the temple are gods? The answer evidently was No; the idol is symbolic of an avatar of God or rather *Paramatma*. That means the idol is God's proxy to enable the Hindu to focus his attention while worshipping. I could not dispute this contention. Well then, for us Muslims, or at least some of us, Pakistan is a proxy for an Islamic state of our hearts desire. Mirza continued by saying that even he felt glad when Pakistan won something but not necessarily at the cost of India. He claimed that the same Muslims celebrated a Pak victory with equal zest even if it was against the West Indies or Australia. Did not Hindu citizens of Britain applaud the Indian team playing against the MCC? The British did not appear to object to the applause, he added.

What earthly use was Pakistan to the Indian Muslim? In fact, the partition had put him at a disadvantage. Many of the elite had migrated leaving behind the rest of the community. Moreover, on the whole subcontinent, the Muslims were a much larger, more influential minority. In 1947, they were divided into two. In 1971, they got trifurcated into three when Bangladesh seceded from Pakistan. Might be so, Mirza replied. But supposing two brothers find themselves surrounded, and only one can escape, should he not go? Or should they take the stand that either both go or neither? And for the chap who remains behind, there is the satisfaction that his brother has founded an Islamic *jamhuriyat*.

Such commitment, even when conflicting with one's own interest, to the brotherhood and to the idea of an Islamic state seemed astonishing to a Hindu. I could not imagine that such altruism could be a reality especially when one considers that the sentiment was not confined to my Urdu teacher. It must be widespread; otherwise how could one explain the many Islamic triumphs? I am yet to meet a single Muslim who has admitted to me that Pakistan was a mistake. If self-interest was the consideration, there is no doubt that the partition divided the subcontinental *ummah* and left it weaker. Evidently the loyalty or the attachment to the dream of a Nizam-e-Mustafa, even if in a different country, overrides an Indian Muslim's self-interest. How very admirable!

One winter morning Mirza came to the house as usual but he looked angry and sullen. I happened to be free so I ordered tea which he had. He became relaxed enough to speak up. I took him up to the first floor verandah where we could be by ourselves and he could unburden his anguish. One of his neighbours at Feroze Shah Road had annoyed him over a bucket of hot water. The neighbour happened to be an orthodox (bigoted according to my teacher) Hindu. The details of the incidence over, Mirza asked if he could tell me something frankly. Go ahead was my response. Let me tell you quite frankly, Mirza began, you Hindus just do not understand us Muslims. What is even sadder is that you have no interest in understanding us either. You hardly ever let us into your homes. You do not eat with us. You never listen to us. You educated Hindus pose as secular but stop short of any real interaction. Politicians flatter our leaders and coax us into voting for them. Behind our backs you hate us because you are mortally afraid of a bogey called the Musalman.

Do you know we do not hate Hindus, he went on. We pity them because they are soft, self-centred and narrow-minded. It is for their good that we try to persuade them to accept and become Muslim. When I raised the question of forcible conversions, Mirza conceded that temptation of jobs and patronage might have been used to convert during medieval times but certainly no force. What about iconoclasts like Mahmud of Ghazni? To this his answer was he must have been substantively a robber and incidentally a Muslim. He destroyed idols in the temples, looted what was hidden below and went away. He did not stay back either to conquer, to rule or to convert Hindus to Islam. Did he?

How would you explain the phenomenon of the Quwwatul-Islam mosque near the Qutab Minar? A large part of it is built with stone pieces which evidently belonged to a Hindu temple. Why such desecration, insult and abuse? I asked. To which Mirza gave what to me then seemed a very interesting, although an ironic explanation. How else could Muhammad Ghori announce to the people of Delhi that he had replaced the rajah as the sultan? Imagine the unavailability of most means of communication at the turn of the twelfth/thirteenth century. Replacing a popular temple with a mosque was about the only authoritative way of doing it. Whenever and whoever came to pray at the temple from the surrounding or the distant places got the message with a bang. I read a similar explanation in a book about the time the Babri edifice at Ayodhya heated up as a controversy. But that was nearly a decade later.

According to Mirza, the desecration (he used the word demolition or replacement) of temples was almost entirely to do with power and little to do with religion. Only the popular prominent temples were affected. The peripheral ones were left alone because they were not as useful as means of communication. I was unhappy with this callous explanation and went on to try to negate my teacher's argument. What was Aurangzeb trying to announce when he desecrated the several temples at Banaras, Mathura and other places? By then the Mughal dynasty had been well ensconced in power for a century and a half.

Aurangzeb was the only one among the Mughals who was at once a ruler and a missionary. He was a devout Muslim and dead set against idol worship. He felt it was his mission to rescue the idol worshippers from heading for *jahannum* or hell, make them accept the final message of Allah as conveyed by his last prophet thus giving them an opportunity of going to *jannat* or paradise instead. His reintroduction of *jizya* or a tax on *kafirs* or infidels was another of his ways of inducing Hindus to cross over to Islam. But even Aurangzeb did not use force, emphasised Mirza. Had he done so the subcontinent could not have remained a Hindu-majority area? Knowing the oppressions of the caste system, do you not agree that 75 percent of the Hindus were sitting ducks for the arrows of Islamic proselytising? These were the outcastes, then called Harijans, now Dalits, plus all the Shudras. The upper castes of Brahmins, Kshatriyas and Vaishyas comprised less than 25 percent of all Hindus.

It was a long day interrupted only by lunch, tea and a few business calls. My curiosity to know and understand more was whetted but its satisfaction had to wait for another day. The suitable day took months to arrive but it did on a Sunday when my wife was away in Bombay. We began at breakfast; the omelette had put him in a good mood.

He began by swearing that a Muslim loved his land dearly, at least as dearly as a Hindu. Perhaps more so, because he expected to be buried in it. And where he is buried is important to a Muslim. He would like to choose his grave if he could afford to do so. I asked if he had any preference. Certainly, he retorted. "If I die in Delhi, please do your best to have me buried near my revered grandfather".

As chance would have it, a couple of years later Mirza died of a severe heart attack in his quarter. His job in the Congress Party office came in handy. Ahmed Patel, the general secretary of the party took special interest and, after considerable effort, a space was located about ten feet from the grandfather's grave. In a nearby mosque, the body was bathed, perfumed, wrapped in a new white cloth and got ready for the final goodbye. At about 10 pm, the *maulvi* read the prayers and the remains of Agha Iqbal Mirza were buried. His younger brother and sister had come from Calcutta to be present. Also present to honour my departed Urdu teacher were Ahmed Patel and Jitendra Prasada, who later became the treasurer and also vice-president of the Congress Party. What Mirza had missed in life he made up by the glory of his funeral!

For me, the whole experience was an eye-opener. I had never before imagined that a dead body could be treated so well, even better than in life. I had seen, as a child, Christian funerals on Girgaum Road in Mumbai from the distance of my grandfather's verandah. The mourners were dressed in their Sunday best. The coffin was immaculate and the body was dressed also in its Sunday best. A band played until the body was placed on the hearse. The Muslim tribute was equally handsome as I saw during Mirza's last journey.

I had been to two or three Hindu and Jain funerals. No dishonour was done to the body but ceremony was absent and there was a hurry to cremate the departed. It is the Hindu view that once the soul or *jeevatma* leaves, the body becomes waste matter. The belief in the transmigration makes the soul all important and the body no more significant than clothes.

In the Judaic or Muslim scheme of thinking there is only one life. There is, therefore, greater importance attached to it. By the same token, death has a finality. The best possible is done for the body until it is returned to the earth. The soul then waits for *qayamat* or doomsday when God would decide who deserves to go to heaven or paradise and who should be consigned to hell or purgatory. When would *doomsday* come? I had once asked Mirza. No one knows, was Mirza's answer. That was why Muhammad was the last prophet who had delivered the final message of God. There was to be no further message or real change until doomsday. And there was also no question of another prophet; there was simply no need.

Sometime earlier there had been tension in Pakistan over the Ahmediya sect which had been declared as non-Muslim. Mirza recalled this issue to illustrate his contention. This denomination was derecognised not for any doctrinal difference but because its founder Mirza Ghulam Ahmad had claimed to be a *paigambar* (messiah) with a newer message of God. That was sacrilege for it contradicted the absolute Muslim belief that Muhammad was the last prophet. There were many Muslim sects that had differences with one another, continued Mirza. The Sunni-Shia rivalry was legend but never has any Sunni (he was one) alleged that the Shias were not Muslim. Their faith in the message delivered by Prophet Muhammad was total. There could be no revision or amendment or a fresh message.

I was surprised. How would the faithful Muslims progress then? The world was changing more rapidly than ever before. How could a prescription, however perfect, given 1,400 years ago still hold good in absolute totality? Surely there had to be some revision, some adjustment? To my questions, Mirza had responded with two simple points. One, the message was not a human creation. It was divine, that of Allah. Two, it was comprehensive and eternal for it dealt with virtually all aspects of life, forever. It was not confined to prayer, worship or ritual. The Holy Quran is not merely a religious text. It is a code of how to lead a good life perennially.

Would that not put Muslims at a disadvantage? To the contrary, Mirza asserted. Is not the faith with which Muslims live and work unique? About the only comparable parallel could be the Jews. The Christians are so dispersed in their effort, so much so that many a Protestant in Europe and America is supposed to have lost interest in Christianity, religion and God. The Roman Catholics were much more sensible although the Pope should not have permitted the Reformation. That was the beginning of the Christian disintegration you witness now. Rebels like Calvin and Luther openly defied the Pope and yet they were not banned from calling themselves Christians. That was no way to run a faith. Another mistake might have been for the Pope not to assume temporal powers over Christendom.

The Hindu impression is that the Muslim is usually not a nationalist, I had said, and anyone like Abul Kalam Azad who placed a priority on his country and its integrity had few Muslim followers. What do you mean by a nationalist? Someone who loves his country? If that be so, most Muslims are nationalist, Mirza asserted. Do you mean their first loyalty is to their country? I enquired. No, between country and religion, Islam usually commands a priority. In fact, for a devout Muslim, his religion is his overriding priority.

Which Hindu can claim that his motherland is everything to him? Does even the most patriotic Hindu love his Hindustan more than his *family*? Would he rather die fighting than abandon his *matribhoomi* if such a desperate dilemma confronted him? In any case, could I claim that all Hindus are nationalists or patriots?

In feudal times, the political loyalty was to the feudal master or lord, in tribal times to the tribe and so on. At least the Muslims have been consistent for 1,400 years. For them Islam is above all, always. But being loyal to Islam does not mean being disloyal or against India. Is your argument then the same as that of the Jews? I enquired. That they were unnecessarily persecuted by the Nazis and the other Semites? No, said Mirza, the Jews have no mission. They do not try to convert non-Jews and bring them closer to God. The Muslims are opposite in this regard. They do their best to bring as many non-believers into their fold as possible. They have a universal mission.

Mirza often repeated that there should be justice towards all religions. I could not really figure out how he could defend, albeit half-heartedly, the reintroduction of *jizya* by Aurangzeb and yet talk about this justice.

He was, however, consistently clear that secularism or the separation of the state from the church was un-Islamic. Prophet Muhammad was at once the spiritual and the temporal head of Islam. The *khalifas* or the caliphs who followed him as his representatives were also popes and kings rolled into one. The Holy Quran was a spiritual as well as a temporal message. Secularism was a Christian and a European concept but a contradiction of Islam. There was no word or term in either Arabic or Urdu for the concept.